Guinn...

See Olympic Records

1896 - 1960

page 86

# THE TORCH WITHIN

# THE
# TORCH
# WITHIN

## EILEEN ROSE

DOUBLEDAY & COMPANY, INC.

GARDEN CITY, NEW YORK

1965

Library of Congress Catalog Card Number 65-11803
Copyright © 1965 by Doubleday & Company, Inc.
Printed in the United States of America
First Edition

To my husband, who has been the perfect companion—
and the son who made motherhood truly blessed

# CONTENTS

"If you have built castles in the air, your work need not be lost; that is where they should be. Now get the foundations under them."

Thoreau

# PREFACE

We have all had a picture of things we want to do—the persons we want to be. What has become of that picture? Was it put away as too good to be true? Then it is time to take it out again and hold it clearly in front of you. Reach out for it! Plan and work for it! Bring it nearer to you every day! You build your own life—*only you!* The materials are all there. Remember, there's never been a truly great person who wasn't once an untried, immature little child. Each of us is capable of so much more. Great things, if we so wish. There are unlimited, untapped powers in reach—yet how few of us take those first steps to something better than our usual mediocre selves!

Though this is the story of Murray, our son, it could just as well be the story of any youngster you have in your mind or heart. It is essentially a story showing that those castles we build in the air can—and should—be formed into a wonderful reality.

This book is concerned largely with sport, especially with swimming, because that was the first medium through which Murray chose to express himself. It was through this that he was able to rise above many early difficulties and prove the power of faith and love and courage.

But as you read and apply the principles to yourself, don't think only of swimming . . . or even of sport. Choose any medium that comes naturally to you or your child. We confidently send out thoughts to all who would enrich their lives, and the lives of their children—especially to those with a problem: a frail body, a nervous temperament, or any imperfection which they wish to overcome. If the desire is great enough, you will find the energy, ability, and inspiration to make those wishes come true. The greatest strength can grow from weakness.

I believe that our story is the story of champions everywhere, great and small, those who have gone and those yet to come. For surely the qualities and forces, the struggles and triumphs that shaped Murray's early life belong to ALL champions. Each leaves a part of himself behind, a measure of inspiration. In the case of our son, it is gratifying to remember that for all time he will remain:

1. The first competitor in the history of the modern Olympic games to win three gold medals at the age of seventeen.

2. The first swimmer ever to win a distance event in two successive Olympics.

3. The first to have broken the eighteen-minute barrier in the 1500-meter swimming marathon, though, as happens in every sport, once a barrier is broken it is no longer there for those who come after.

He created his first world record in 1956. Since then he has held most world records over the middle distance and long distance events—and he is still a world-record holder today, eight years later.

And, for our own record, he championed a personal ideal, in that all his swimming feats were accomplished on simple, natural foods as we believe man was intended to live—and without eating animal flesh.

# THE TORCH WITHIN

## CHAPTER 1

# LIGHTING THE TORCH

I remember, as a little girl, being fascinated by the picture of an Olympic champion, and how I was drawn to this symbol of perfect manhood until it became almost a living part of my life. When school friends reached the stage of dreams and pinned up screen-star pictures around their rooms, I could never find a hero to replace this Olympic ideal.

"How wonderful it would be," I once said to my mother, "for two people to have a son who would become a great Olympic champion. I can think of no greater goal." Though perhaps not conscious of the power of my thoughts, some design for the future was surely taking shape.

Certainly I developed an interest in the stories of ancient Greece, and was inspired by accounts of the stirring victory ceremonies and the Olympic champions' feats; catching something, perhaps, of their reverence for a disciplined mind and a perfected physique. We cannot know just how and when our thoughts will build themselves around us, but I am very sure that it is we ourselves who really do the building.

Each of us lives through a drama very much of our own making—a drama we ourselves direct, scene by scene. The joys we draw to us, the pains we suffer, all the good things and all the bad, we give them power by *thinking* them so before they appear as experiences, facts, or wonderful creations.

The beauty of a painting was once a vision in the artist's mind. And the whole structure of a building must be imagined and planned before one brick can appear in its place.

The pattern of our lives is formed in much the same way. The beliefs we allow to take root in our thoughts have a way of shaping themselves around us—invisibly at first and then as realities, exactly in the form we gave them.

There are periods in life, long periods at times, which seem outwardly uneventful, and we feel how little headway we are making. But these are the very times when valuable building is often taking place so long as we are firmly set on becoming perfect in our field, and miss no possible opportunity of coming closer to our dream. If we constantly and silently "see" ourselves in the position, or state, that we know we can fill, feeling all the pleasure and joy as though it were already ours, then only doubts and negative thoughts will prevent it from coming true. Not only the great achievements can be THOUGHT into our lives, but the warm and sweet and necessary things as well.

Up to the time of coming to the United States, our Olympic story had filled much of our lives and thoughts. It had brought long journeys, and many changes, and left little opportunity for planning a permanent home. But five years ago I thought it was time to start building one in my heart. And the place I envisioned as perfect for us appeared in a most unusual way. Today it is a solid and very lovely fact.

In the quietude of a hidden corner in the Hollywood Hills, I take up this story already left unfinished for far too long. It was the message of a newscaster which sparked me off again.

"Tonight in Los Altos," came the voice over the air, "Murray Rose, one of the greatest swimmers of all time made a new world record in the 800-meters freestyle event—this being his third world and fourth American record during the last two weeks. Murray, recently honored as the outstanding graduating athlete from the University of Southern California, had barely a month's training under his belt—"

Barely a month's training? More like twenty years. It had all begun a long time ago when two tiny, plump legs had staggered uncertainly into the sea—and reached a first big climax at the XVI Olympiad at Melbourne.

As I remembered, the lights of the city of Los Angeles beneath our windows were changing into other lights— lights reflected and leaping in the churning waters of a pool. And there I was again in this place made so vivid by much mental revisiting. I could smell its damp warmth and see the many faces unchangingly impressed by the impact of that night's experience. I became tense with anxiety; barely able to look at the great Olympic swimming marathon being battled out in the water below . . . thirty strenuous laps in which each of the main place-getters had fought his way, for a while, into the lead. Now the last powerful strokes were being swum, and tired bodies strained for that final ounce of strength—and, if possible, a strength beyond that.

Suddenly it was all over. The excited crowd was on its feet sending roar upon roar around the stadium until a fair, very young man shyly ascended the dais to receive his third gold medal at this, the XVI Olympiad. I watched while, in his honor, the standard of his country was being raised, and I knew a moment of overwhelming gratitude and pride—an indelible moment of seeing a son earn and reach for his first great goal.

During the emotional aftermath of well-wishing and handclasps, there was one incident which left me wondering. Among those who came to offer congratulations was the coach of one of the great American universities. We sat apart for a while discussing the many facets of sport, and exchanging views on the essentials necessary in the building of any athletic star; the training, diet, self-discipline, and the tremendous hard grind.

Quite suddenly he posed this pretty big question. "I wonder," he said, "whether you could supply the clue for which I've been searching through all the years of my coaching career? What *is* it that gives that little extra something changing an ordinary human being into someone special? What makes a fine athlete into a world champion? What *is* that undefined quality behind the truly great?"

Perhaps the answer as to what provides that touch of greatness, that little extra so necessary in the final test, lies in the goal itself. Is it a big enough one to overcome all obstacles? Is it worthy of prayer? Can we remove all fear and belief in limitation? And are we able to contact God's ever present power for help and inspiration—to "tune-in," as it were, and let it work through and with us? Surely there is no other way to develop a never ending stream of strength and courage within, to add that "little extra."

There are many success stories that wonderfully illustrate this. Men and women who faced great difficulties before rising to places of honor and fame. The motive behind their strivings is invariably a brave and noble one. Some are governed by a deep love of country, while others seek to overcome a weakness of mind or body and so point the way to many without hope. There is a quality in the "great" which is beyond self-seeking: a faith which brings them a sort of passport to God. Humility and gentleness are theirs, too, for they are aware that all strength comes from a power beyond their own. There must be a never ending striving towards goals of true value in order to reach that "extra help."

The glamour of being a public hero, the excitement and thrilling moments of success are very obvious rewards. But the question which so often arises, when people discover the tremendous hard work behind the scenes, is whether it has all been truly worthwhile. They see the life of discipline and dedicated thought not only demanded of the champion himself but, in some measure, by those close to him, for it is vital, in the beginning years especially, to plan, encourage, and give down-to-earth support.

During periods of challenge, disappointment, and strain we have naturally been faced with such questions ourselves. We have weighed ephemeral pleasures against lasting benefits . . . the prickings of doubt against an inner belief, and the very human desire to just "sit in the sun" against the realization that this gets no one anywhere.

So the answer must come sincerely from our hearts. Yes, it has all been very much worthwhile, for it was not only an athletic star in the making—but a man with a promise— and birthright—of great fulfillment.

It was, I believe, Bob Kiphuth, the "father of swimming" and famous Yale coach, who once remarked, "Show me a great champion and you show me a person of character and determination, one who has practiced self-discipline and control, who can take a beating and be the better for the lesson—a man who inspires respect and admiration, who will surely get places, not only in sport, but in any other field of life he chooses. For such a one learns early the rules of life and is able to apply them in any game."

Who could regret working to bring about a result such as this?

We all of us hope for something very special for our children—and why not? I am sure that it is possible to make a champion of any one of them; or rather help them to reach the top in whatever field suits them best. Aiming for the top simply must mean a change, and an effort—but that's all in the molding of the metal. And I've yet to meet the parent who wouldn't gladly give a pretty big slice of himself in helping a dream to come true. Dream? Better make it goal and be sure of a solid foundation.

There's nothing like a challenge to bring real meaning

and new horizons into our lives. How afraid most of us are
of changing the patterns we know, or of attempting to see
things from any different point of view. How often do we
give our inner voice a "hearing"? Or challenge those "sec-
ondhand" opinions that have us hypnotized into believing
they are our own? How much of ourselves do we squander
by spending so many hours under the hypnotic spell of
radio and TV? We have so much potential, such a wealth
of "built-in" wisdom—and so little time in which to uncover
it all and put it to good use.

Only *we* can fulfill every promise to ourselves. Just as
soon as we look for the answers to the One Source of Wisdom, innate within each one of us, and allow ourselves to be
guided and sustained by faith, then everything begins to
change. Helpful, strengthening thoughts will be ours to be
set into action. Self-imposed limitations will slip away. The
feelings of others towards us will be warmly changed, and
the conditions of our whole life will take on a wonderfully
different shape. Put it to the test for a day—even for an
hour!

Forget the self you've become used to and look at everything as "someone new" who has just arrived. See the good
(which is God) in all things, all people. Give them your
whole interest and loving attention. You might be amazed
at the transformation this can bring. Try it! It really works.

When afraid to face up to some new challenge, I remember the courage exemplified by the little fledgling that had
outgrown its shell and eaten all the food within that small
space. Had it been afraid to break its shell and face up to a
strange and unknown world, it would have surely perished,
whereas once it broke free it quickly grew strong enough to
soar above all that had been confining.

At the time we found ourselves on the opposite side of
the world from our own dear homeland, there seemed
change enough to be faced. Perhaps the enthusiasm of

youth had invited fresh experiences for challenge after challenge came our way. It was surprising, even to us, that a whole new way of living and thinking should come upon us almost overnight. This was the time *we* broke through our "eggshell," for although it brought something of a revolution into our home and habits, we felt no regret at seeing the old things go. There was a meaning to life we had never seen there before—enriching new channels of interest and thought, bringing "treasures to seek within, as well as without."

But in taking a road that is different from the majority's there are barriers to break down, misunderstandings to be met, and a host of critics, skeptics, and doubters all the way. However, enthusiasm is catching, we soon found out, while sincerity—*plus success*—wins over in the end.

When Murray first arrived in California to begin his college career, his fame as an athlete had preceded him. Being interviewed on several TV programs, he found himself under a barrage of fire and facing many challenging questions. Wasn't it a great strain permanently to discipline himself in order to become a great champion? Didn't he miss this food or that? What were the psychological effects of the life he had led? Did it cause repression and frustrations?

Murray's answers came easily and were firmly reassuring that once a habit is formed, especially a lifelong habit such as his, then it comes naturally and without any feeling of strain or frustration. A way of life is what you like to make it. It is all so much in the mind—a matter of conditioning. Your way of life *is* you!

## CHAPTER 2

## SETTING THE GOAL

Right from the start Murray's guardian angel must have been there on the job, for without predetermination on our part he was led safely away from the dark world to which he'd been born. Instead of growing up in freedom on the sun-flooded beaches of Australia, he might so easily have known the fear and privations of a war-tormented city in the danger zones of the English Midlands.

How many little ones coming to earth around that time and place must have found it a home of shuddering sounds, of buildings crashing about them, of mutilations, death, and the sudden loss of loving protection! As it was, with the bells of Christmas 1939 echoing in our ears, we slipped quietly away from the foggy coast line of England. Even then, at eleven months, Murray seemed to sense the job that awaited him down under. Impatient at the long delay caused by rigid wartime precautions, he grabbed the emigration officer's rubber stamp and attempted to okay the passports himself—eager as it were, to catch up with destiny!

### The Start of a Dream

The thoughts that started the pattern of Murray's way of life must have begun many years before.

It was in the green loveliness of the English countryside

that both my husband and I had received our early conditioning. We grew up, as do country children everywhere, in close touch with the simple, rhythmic beauty of nature's laws. Mine was the enchanted world Walt Disney tries to capture. And in the secrets of tangled hedgerows and narrow winding lanes, nature herself became my teacher.

Out on wild moors and under the mystic spell of forests she showed me the beauty and strength that grows out of gentle persistence—and she tuned my ears to wisdom whispering through the timeless humming of meadows. Her abundant goodness and changeless laws formed golden rules that I never quite forgot for she spoke the language that children understand. I learned of love in its truest form, and much of pain and cruelty too, as well as something of the infinite unchangeable laws, and the urge behind all earthly striving.

There were wild creatures of every kind living in my playground, and that close contact with the animal world brought a warm feeling of lasting friendship. I caught their vibrant acceptance of "being" and of squeezing every ounce of life, from each moment, as it comes. I enjoyed their fun and loved their courage and grieved for their suffering.

The Oneness of Life became very clear, and though I could not have expressed it in words, I knew that One Mind had formed all things and put them here as a part of some wise but incomprehensible plan—a plan in which all life shares and is lovingly guided to grow through experience.

What an easy happiness came from "little things," then! The springtime discovery of the first bird's eggs, and violets peering through long grass; the amusing awkwardness of a newly born foal, and tiny lambs like soft white balls bouncing and leaping in an ecstasy of living. But there the picture ended, for I would be taken home to dinner and offered a generous portion of new-season's lamb—killed and cooked merely for our "pleasure."

I remember becoming deeply troubled and confused on suddenly becoming aware of the inconsistencies of grown-ups who seemed blandly to accept a strange double set of values. And my baffled parents, completely assured of their own right thinking and humane behavior, would vainly try to end the tears by explaining the unexplainable.

There must be many imaginative, sensitive children who are faced with this same puzzle, children imbued with love and compassion from the adults around them, but who must accept without question the need for cruelty and pain.

Somehow the delight of being a child was never quite the same again, for the contradictions of "love" had been uncovered, and I sought to understand the reason for so much unnecessary suffering.

It was about then that an incident occurred which was so filled with horror that every shocking detail still remains in my mind. This might well have been the moment that set the pattern of my grown-up life, though I could not have been more than five years old at the time.

In small English towns and villages, it was the custom to keep animals at the back of butchers' shops and slaughter them on the premises. How I came to be in one of those shops, I do not remember, but I was there and being held by an elder child and forced to watch while a terrified pig was being chased and caught. Terrible hooks were put through its hinds legs, and, shrieking in agony and fear, it was hauled upside down on a pulley and its throat cut. Then it was slit open, all the way down. The sight, smell, and sound of that incident was so ghastly that I was paralyzed with terror. This was no doubt the moment that caused me to give up eating meat many years later.

Only recently I met a strong giant of a man whose whole life had also been colored by a similar childhood event. It seems that as a very small boy, he had owned a pet chicken, which he loved and cared for and believed to be his very own. Coming into the garden one day, he was just in time to see his grandmother cutting off the head of the shrieking bird, and he watched, horrified, while the poor, decapitated creature ran for a while with only a body. He too lives as we do today and eats no animal products. As he is a successful and popular football player by profession, it was all the more surprising to associate him with such a background.

This is surely a most convincing proof that it is neither weak nor unmanly to show reverence and feeling towards all life. It frequently calls for the greatest of courage. Today we have people like Albert Schweitzer who dedicate their all to such a cause. Then, there was One called Jesus, Who exemplified the same ideals nearly two thousand years ago, while the gentle strength of St. Francis of Assisi is remembered in the prayers of millions.

The fact that I lived in a famous hunting district made further conflictions of thought an everyday affair. Kindly, lovable people, often my friends and family, would put on their scarlet coats and behave like mad things, or show the same hysteria as that induced by the beating of a native war drum.

I felt deeply for the fox, whose means of survival is so exactly the same as most living creatures. Why, I wondered, was he chosen to be the victim of such extraordinary cruelty. There were many evenings that I thought of this as I saw him on guard close to his family, his coat gleaming a deep red in the light of the setting sun—always alert and so afraid.

Was the instinct to eat and "take home" a good dinner really so great a crime? Did it warrant the long ordeal and unbearable pain which was so frequently his lot? On days when I heard the hunter's horn, I knew just how the fox must feel. Why should this crowd of grown men and hungry dogs chase one small, terrified animal—keeping it up for hours if need be, until, exhausted, he'd be caught and torn to pieces while still alive?

When asked, the huntsmen reason that this is "true sport," and besides, they are doing the farmers a great service by protecting their young animals and poultry. But protecting them from what? Aren't these same animals preserved merely to be killed by men instead of the fox?

Near my home, as in most country districts in England, there was the usual titled landowner who kept large areas of beauty fenced off. Not in order that he might go there alone to quietly refresh his soul, nor even for relaxation after a gay London season. But purely as an area where bird and animal life would be protected, so that when the mood suited him, he and his friends could be sure of enough living targets for a good day's fun.

I can feel again the "forbidden" magic of those woods where trespassing steps were silenced by the deep, springy moss that covered the paths. And where primroses would be sprinkled by the way, like so many patches of moonlight, caught and held there from the night before. Here, surely, were the signs of fairy folk—who knows—if I could creep a little further in! Suddenly the harsh voice of a gamekeeper would shatter the quiet, and running back, frightened, I would hear the whirr of strong wings and catch the vivid flash of blue and green as a pheasant rose from near my feet. Would there soon be a shot, telling me that all that vibrant warmth had fallen back to earth—a deep red stain on those glossy feathers?

On the days when I brought tidbits to my friends on the lake—the swans, water fowl and ducks—the story would so often end the same. Nothing and no one (least of all, a little child) should be allowed to disturb the shooting pleasures of his lordship and his guests.

But sometimes I was lucky as I walked through the fields, and came across a trap already set—but empty. With what deep satisfaction I would release the cruel spring before it had a chance of breaking some fragile little limb, or of holding a tortured body in many hours of pain.

Did this cruelty have to be? Was there something that could be done? Living in a world so filled with beauty and surrounded by the warmth of human tenderness, it is hard for the seeking child to understand the real meaning of truth and love. So a little girl wondered and worried and longed to help. Her prayers must have been heard, for many years later she was shown the way.

## Born on a Prayer

It was in a strange new land that I found the answer to this childhood dream. But first I had to meet my prince, who wasn't a prince at all but a mercurially minded advertising man from London, tall and handsome enough and possessing all the keen, probing faculties associated with his profession, but with a sensibility, too, that guided him through to find the good, and beautiful, and true. He was nothing whatever of an athlete, for he wasn't even strong; part of his inheritance had been that of ill-health, for a childhood illness had left him with a badly damaged heart. However, he shared my feelings for the natural and simple things, loving nothing better than to walk, talk, and think in the quiet of country places. In short, I was loved and fell in love.

Was it mere coincidence that we married in sight of the sea, that element which has since played such a part in the molding of our lives, or that our wedding march came from the rythmic sound of the surf as it washed unceasingly over the pebbles of a Sussex beach?

The day of January 6, 1939, was quite a history-making one for us. I remember it all in vivid detail. Everything glistened white around our home in Birmingham, England, and our fir trees drooped under a heavy weight of snow. The gathering clouds were not only of nature's making for the threat of war also hung darkly in the air. It was not the happy world we would have chosen for our son's arrival here but this was the day he chose anyway.

As I was drowsing under the effect of chloroform, I remember a flight of fighter planes thundering past, and my thoughts were all of a gentler, happier way of life for the little one on its way. I must have been murmuring while half asleep, for the doctor was saying as I came round, "This child has come in on a prayer, nurse, I think we should add our blessings too." I looked out of the window, and there was now no sight nor sound suggestive of war— only one bright star faintly appearing in the quickly darkening sky.

He was quite small at first and not exceptionally strong. Ian, very much aware of his own physical background, wished only the happiness of health for his son.

We lived at that time in an old Georgian house, whose elegance might once have been impressively grand, but now it was tired and very old-fashioned. Though bright coals burned in every fireplace, we could never discourage the winter chills from creeping around those spacious rooms. And its fading affluence brought a feeling of false security. There was always a sense of unreality about our stay there, rather as though we moved in some romantic play, which we knew must soon come to an end. With the spring, came a beauty that could never fade or date, for the daffodils gathered under the trees, and the crocuses on the lawn. Climbing roses of summertime hid the crumbling garden walls, while crowding the wide borders were lilies and marigolds, hollyhock and larkspur, and the sweet, trusting faces of a thousand pansies.

Murray's christening brought a gathering of the clan, for

it was both a gala and Gaelic affair; his ancestors on the
paternal side being descendants from an unbroken line of
Highland Scots. His first name, Iain, was given the Gaelic
spelling in honor of these stalwart forebears of the Clan
Rose who had fought for Bonnie Prince Charlie and the
Royalist cause and whose plaid was seen on the battlefield
of Cullodon Moor in 1746. An old family home built among
the glens of Morayshire gave him the well-known "Murray"
part of his name.

Grandfather Rose, one of the first of his clan to live
among the "heathen" south of the Scottish border, had
always retained the stamp of the kilt, while his warm,
lilting brogue held the music of heather.

My own parents, too, had joined the celebrations, coming
from their home near Sherwood Forest, that much fabled
greenwood, renowned as the hideaway of one Robin Hood.

The rejoicing was real enough, for this, the first grand-
child on both sides of the family.

The clergyman who officiated lived in the house next
door, and during the tense days which followed, he would
quietly stroll in for a chat and a cup of tea in the garden.
As our thoughts were never far from the impending world
crisis, he tried to imbue us with his own deep faith—"There
is always a Loving Help to show us the way of His Plan,"
and he would quietly smile down at Murray kicking, unperturbed, in his pram.

We made one big mistake in those early days—the most
unfortunate one of having Murray vaccinated—though the
full significance of our error was not brought home to us
until several years later. Like most young parents we
wanted only to love and protect our baby, but sentimen-
tality is very far from enough. Had we made every effort to
acquire greater wisdom, we could undoubtedly have done
a better job. But we left decisions, too important to be taken

lightly, to the judgment of orthodox "authorities." The whole idea of vaccination had instinctively repulsed me.

Why entertain thoughts of sickness in a tiny, pure body, let alone *put* it there by forcibly introducing the lymph of a diseased animal? The natural law of Cause and Effect can never be circumvented, and this is surely setting it in motion the wrong way round, both in thought and action.

At the time that our doctor insisted on vaccination I had only emotional antipathy to combat his arguments. I did not have the backing of scientific facts and overwhelming figures to set against the weight of medical jargon and confusing technicalities.

How hard to strip off years of conventional impression and to view such a matter with clear insight! Ian himself believed it only right for Murray to have the "blessings" of modern medicine, though now, after years of research and study, he gives much of his time and energy to publicly opposing the vaccine theory. He wrote of this in his book *Faith, Love and Seaweed.*

I grieved at the inner knowledge that we were doing wrong and was sick at heart when I heard Murray's cries and saw the two ugly suppurating outbreaks on that perfect little arm. There is no excuse for ignorance. It was our job to have been well armed against such wrong thinking. But even mistakes can be of value in showing the way to better things.

Such strange thoughts and unorthodox ideas would undoubtedly have shocked Murray's conventional old French "nanny," encased as she was in the lifelong impressions firmly fixed by her "superiors." However, she was devoted to her charge—almost fanatically so—and when she first took over, we believed her to be a real "treasure."

At first my visits to the nursery were wonderfully happy times for naturally I loved most in the world to be with our little Iain Murray, as we affectionately called him then.

Quite a strict conditioning program was planned right from the start, and we both enjoyed the daily routine of his gentle baby calisthenics, a thorough massage with almond oil, and then out into the garden for his regular bath of air and sunshine. Even in England's hesitant sun he quickly grew strong and firm and gloriously brown.

But then we noticed something strange about this adoring old nurse. With subtle suggestions and old wives' tales, she tried to upset me when I handled our child. In fact, her weird fancies and ominous premonitions soon had me frightened and deeply disturbed, changing my joy into nervous apprehension. Our doctor called it motherhood frustration causing jealous resentment and a malicious desire to separate me from our beloved wee son. He took a most serious view of the unnatural situation and insisted that she must go. After many painful and emotional scenes she was finally replaced by a young and starched machine, straight from a nursing college—kind, efficient, and wholesomely normal.

As it happened, however, the violence of war was to part us from Murray anyway. For too short a time we knew great content, and the last rays of peace were as poignantly warm as those of any setting sun.

In many ways this was a fairy-story time.

When war was officially declared on September 3, 1939, it disrupted the home life of most English families. It jolted us right out of ours. Birmingham being in the center of England's munition industry, it became imperative that Murray be moved to a safer place. Seemingly impossible decisions followed, one after another. I resolved to stay behind with Ian, and, numbly bewildered, we arranged for nurse and baby to go to the greater safety of the countryside.

Still stunned from Neville Chamberlain's declaration and the pitiful upheaval of our united little world, I instinctively peeped into the empty nursery, looking for comfort at the spot where my son should now be taking his morning bath. But no baby chuckles warmed my heart. The phone rang, and the last thin wall of security went down. It was Ian's voice telling me of his resignation from the advertising agency where he worked. Not only because of the vulnerability of our home, but because of the lack of principle demonstrated in the office. His chief, knowing the effect that war might have on his business, was immediately firing all of the older men: men who had faithfully spent their lives in his service. Integrity and loyalty are the very fiber of Ian's make-up, and he wanted no part of such ruthless behavior.

During the sad task of packing and preparing to leave the home to which we knew we should never return, I ran a constant temperature of 103 degrees, apparently for no other reason than a bad case of heartache.

Mabel, our devoted little maid, had tears running down her country-pink cheeks, as she shyly offered her farewell gift, a giant box of candies for which she had undoubtedly dipped deep into her week's wages.

"I'll put in more daffodils for the spring, mum, never fear," said Old Joe, the gardener, as we took his hand in warm gratitude.

We were all playing a part, desiring vainly to hang on to the quiet order of things we had happily shared together, yet knowing that it had ended for good.

## CHAPTER 3

## NEW HORIZONS

Our future plans were now very much in a chrysalis stage, for we had no way of knowing how or where they would emerge. Making for the center of activity, we stayed with Ian's parents in London.

Ian volunteered for the Scots Guards, but his physical requirements were below the standards of the Highland regiment. He sought to put his creative and writing skill to some practical, useful work and offered his services to the Department of Information and other government offices. But the occupants of such jobs, often men well fitted for active service, were doggedly hanging on; obstinately determined to see the emergency through from their comfortable chairs in Whitehall. It was, at that time, impossible to break into their magic circle.

Murray was being cared for in one of the "Stately Old Homes of England," and only once during the following tense months could we make the difficult journey to see him. The visit brought only a further anxiety, for a new regimen had been formed, and we had become complete strangers to him. Without supervision and insistence on the natural, hardy program we believed so valuable, his habit of exercise and exposure to open air had been replaced by a coddled, overdressed existence, while an overdose of milk and starchy processed foods was putting on unnatural weight and destroying his vitality. Maybe he was protected from outside attack, but not so from well-meaning enemies within. Years of trouble were unwittingly being built during this period. However, he was loved well enough, and as safe as could be from bombs, and for those blessings we were very grateful. But somehow we must, and would, all get together again. Our hearts and plans were centered on that.

We decided to emigrate—somewhere—anywhere! Australia? South Africa? Even the Gold Coast was in our thoughts, for Murray's godfather had begged us to join him there, promising a life of peace and comfort—but what could Ian do in this tropical wilderness?

In a state of great uncertainty as to our next stop, we ran into a friend who declared his interest in astrology and persuaded Ian, much against his own belief at the time, to listen to the analysis of his horoscope.

"There is no doubt that Australia is the place for you," he told Ian, adding, "your son is destined to become a well-known person and of great pride and benefit to his parents."

However, the problems of being allowed to leave a country at war were unbelievingly difficult.

We managed to book a passage on the next available ship sailing for down under and with much patience and pulling of strings obtained every document needed, except the vital exit permit. Time was running out—the ship would soon be sailing. Murray's nurse was leaving to help in a hospital for wounded soldiers. With no home and no job, it was difficult not to panic. Ian spent the best part of every day at the Emigration Department. First one requirement, then another, was demanded. Could we show visible proof of support in Australia, for we were allowed to take very little money from England, even if we had it? In the few days left, how was this to be accomplished? We suddenly remembered a friend who had settled in Australia.

He understood our desperate cable and answered in reply: "AGREE PAY YOU A THOUSAND POUNDS ANNUALLY STOP TAKE CHARGE OF COPY DEPARTMENT ON ARRIVAL IN SYDNEY . . ." This seemed to satisfy the powers that be, but still we waited for final permission to leave England's shores. There was only a matter of hours before the boat would sail without us. Desperately I decided to take over Ian's vigil. A woman's way might change our luck. All through the day I waited, listening hopefully for our name to be called. The doors would soon be closing, and then it would be too late—there was just one chance. Approaching the receptionist's desk, I turned on an attack of nervous hysteria, telling her of our desperate plight. Somehow, I found myself facing the official who would decide our fate. Tears came easily enough as I related our predicament. If only to restore the peace of his office, the poor man gladly signed the precious document and handed me a copy.

At last the day came when an unrecognizable bundle of thick white woolens was handed to us through the boat-train window. And sailing through mine-infested seas on a blacked-out liner, we and our son became acquainted once again.

Coming straight from the clockwork control of his nurse, Murray was a model of baby behavior, and during the long voyage his day's routine was as predictable and easy to run as that of any crew member.

For a time our 20,000-ton liner was a sitting target for the enemy. "Life-jackets must be carried at all times." The peremptory notice posted in dining rooms, bathrooms, and on deck left no doubt as to our course of action. Male passengers took it in turn to volunteer for extra-lookout jobs. The English Channel was a known hunting ground

for German submarines, and just before we reached the
Indian Ocean, we heard that a Nazi pocket battleship had
been seen in this area. Let one tiny spark prick the solid
darkness of our blacked-out liner, and a sharp voice would
jerk us back to the dangers around. "Put out that cigarette!
Are you trying to sink the ship?"

But the spirit of Christmas persisted, in the unquenchable
way it will, and with all the warmth and gaiety of peace-
time cheer, while the first New Year's party that Murray
was on earth to see was as laughter-filled as the ship's
staff and little children could make it.

And so we passed the apprehensive days at sea, but with
us so busy catching up on baby care that we gave little
thought to the likelihood of a long, cold swim.

One night, however, came the inevitable and almost expected warning of danger and the alarming command to
proceed immediately to our allotted boat stations. Rather
dazed, we pulled on warm garments, tied our life jackets
firmly around the waist, and tenderly gathered up the
deeply sleeping Murray. Among the regimented, well-
drilled lines of passengers one felt a curious mixture of fear
and faith. Listening to the ominous sound of lifeboats
being readied and the clipped, over-assured tones of the
ship's officers, one felt pretty close to terror. Looking at
the dark, freezing water brought no hope or comfort whatever. Then, as though pulling my attention to it, I became
aware of one brilliant star—the very same, I liked to think,
as the one I had noticed when Murray was born. Its
brightness reminded me of a strength—a strength beyond
the human endeavors of the crew. All would be well, I was
very sure of that.

And so the danger passed. The shuddering sound of a
direct hit never came, and quietly we all went back to bed.

Each day grew warmer, each wave grew calmer, until,

miraculously protected, we saw Bombay, faint and small on the horizon.

There was a startling quiet as the ship's engines were cut and we felt the presence of India. Domed temples, low, square buildings, and distant hills all merged into the glowing evening sky. We sensed an overpowering stillness as of many minds tuned to the peace of eternity.

In order to hasten the boat through and out of danger, giant flares were set around the hold, and the work of loading and unloading went on through the night. Quick, dancing shapes moved as though in flames, while strange calls and native chatter supplied the eerie sound effects. Brown-skinned figures squatted silently on the wharf as if waiting to take their turn in a scene from Dante's Inferno.

No matter what the hour of day or night that a "sightseeing cargo" arrives in an Indian port, stores are thrown open and every coaxing art of selling is set into motion. In the atmosphere of incense and sad-eyed entreaty, we were as easily disarmed as everyone else, eagerly adding to a growing pile of "bargains"—a silver-spangled sari, bizarre bracelets, and scarves light and gleaming as desert moonbeams. Women ran beside us, holding up puny infants and crying for alms; pitiful beggars brought a feeling of guilt that one was fed and clothed; while children whined incessantly for coins.

We were led from the pungent, chattering street and into the cool, white comfort of the Taj Mahal Hotel. It was here, while sipping ice-cold drinks, that Ian was offered a position with the largest advertising agency in India. We had only a few hours in which to make up our minds.

"What about it?" Ian asked. "Shall we collect Murray and all of our belongings and see how we like it for a while?"

We tried to picture how life would be in Bombay, and we remembered friends who had returned from such a background—spoiled, superficial, and painfully egotistical.

In this rather unnatural, artificial world, might our son grow into an overbearing child? Almost in answer to our thoughts, a little girl walked past, elegantly dressed in bouffant white organdie, her hair brushed and shining with tender care. But then, in harsh, peevish tones we heard:

". . . You do as I say, or I shall complain to my parents . . ." She spoke disdainfully and cruelly to her patient ayah. This was no place for us. We continued our journey, prepared to learn our lessons in a tougher land.

One hot night about this time I had a strange experience of mental telepathy. As there were now empty cabins on the ship, we had acquired a second one in order to take turns at being near Murray through the night. This was Ian's turn to be on duty. I awoke from sleep, hearing Murray calling "Mummy." The fact that he was still too young to talk never crossed my mind. I ran quickly to the other cabin, some distance away. Murray was just falling from his cot, and I managed to break his fall. Such incidents are surely evidence enough of interconnected thought waves which communicate through some super-telephone service all their own.

At Colombo our son took his first journey into a foreign land, and his first look at a Buddhist temple. But his introduction to this saintly teacher was not appreciated then. In deference for the Buddhist belief that any part of a slaughtered animal would desecrate a holy place, all leather footwear must be left outside. As we entered the dim interior, and a yellow-robed priest removed even the baby blue shoes from Murray's small feet, our son obviously began thinking it all very strange. By the time we came in sight of the inner temple, dominated by its immense, be-jeweled figure, he began to sob in fear. But we hastened him back to sunshine and smiles and played with fragrant frangipani flowers which lay strewn about the little holy courtyard.

Perhaps something of the gentle spirit went with us after all, for Eastern thought and metaphysical philosophy have played quite a part in influencing Murray's life.

Back again at sea we found the ship's portholes opened wide. What a wonderful relief! There is nothing like the deprivation of some essential we have taken for granted for its true value to be forced upon us. In this case it was something as simple as pure fresh air. After many nights of tossing in stuffy, airless cabins, we could now enjoy and treasure the tangy salt-filled air. People began to come alive again. They laughed and played and danced under the stars. And Murray had his first tryout in a swimming pool. Our world was free and unrestrained at last.

One morning as we played our daily game of quoits, there was an excited call from someone looking out to sea . . . "An Albatross! Now we must be getting pretty close." A great, weird bird came swooping over the ship, and it stayed alongside for the final part of the voyage.

Australian passengers had tears in their eyes, as hazily from the sea the first shapes of their land began to appear. Someone started humming the Australian national song, "Advance, Australia Fair." One by one others joined in, until it grew into a stirring chorus, and very much a hymn of gratitude.

"Take a good look, mate," said a big and hearty ranch owner, lifting Murray up high. "That's God's own country. But you'll find that out if you grow up there."

There was a rather poignant echo to these sentiments many years later, almost to the day of my writing about them. The ship that had carried us safely to Australia was setting sail on her last voyage before being broken up. And in the correspondence columns of the main Sydney newspaper the following letter appeared:

## SHE BROUGHT US MURRAY

Dear Sir,

The final departure from Australia of the liner *Strathmore* recalls an early wartime visit. On this particular trip she brought to Australia a young Englishman, his wife and their fair-haired infant son.

That baby, whom I saw develop into a sturdy swimmer at Redleaf Pool, became our world-renowned Olympic swimming champion, Murray Rose—a dinkum Aussie! Can't we pack modern liners with future British settlers in our country, of such worth and outstanding value to Australia?

—Kerwin Maegraith, Double Bay.

On the morning of our arrival, some twenty-five years ago, the thing that struck us most was the exceptional brilliance of light. As we first sailed through the famous "heads" which stand at the entrance to the port of Sydney, the landscape colors seemed many shades brighter than the familiar pastel tones of England. Even nature, it seemed, had turned up her lights in welcome.

But as we started down the gangplank on our way to shore, we gasped and drew back. The forceful wind which met us was so intensely hot that it scorched, like the draft from some immense oven—suggestive, perhaps, of the furnace of the Master Potter and the molding process about to begin.

"We expect to stay about eighteen months," we had told our families on leaving England. How could we have ever dreamed that eighteen months would be stretched into eighteen years?

## CHAPTER 4

## OFF TO A FRESH START

Coming from the cold of an English winter straight into the inferno of a Sydney heat wave was by far the warmest part of our welcome down under. Arriving in a country renowned for its good nature and generous attitude towards youth, we were unfortunate, no doubt, in not knowing the doors which were later so willingly opened for us. For a time we were lost and painfully unprepared for the difficulties we met there—mainly on account of the fact that a very small Murray happened to be there too.

In this beautiful but crowded harborside city the better hotels and guesthouses discouraged any visitors with babies, and our attempts to find a place in which to live proved at first to be unavailing. Once again, we were faced with a sad decision and forced to temporarily separate from our tiny son. Having no one to turn to for practical help, we arranged for his care at a privately run nursery while I searched for a home and Ian for a job.

Bright with flowers, built upon hills, with sun-gleaming water a part of every scene, Sydney imparts a gaiety to which one quickly responds. Here we found a carefree spirit that always lifts the heart and an easygoing people whose innate love of freedom inspires an unfettered way of life—a natural reaction, no doubt, from those not-so-distant days of shackles and prison ships.

A constant battle with the elements and a hard fight from

the start has molded the Aussie into a tougher being than most. A natural-born gambler, he takes life in his stride and enjoys each moment fully as it comes. He will give his all to a "cobber" in real need, and you can back him to win through whatever the odds. But after knowing the gentle suavity of an old and mellowed country it comes hard at first to readily adjust to one which is young and less restrained. Indeed the corners will be rather painfully rubbed off before one becomes attuned to the more robust and simplified way of things.

Gradually our pattern evolved, for, after some weeks of hunting, Ian joined a well-known advertising agency, and I discovered a harbor-view home just a few steps away from a deserted little beach—now the over-popular Redleaf Pool.

When we arrived at the nursery to reclaim Murray, for the second time in his short life, he had completely forgotten who we were.

We began to feel like children escaping from some harsh school and longed to share our freedom with those we had left behind in England. How they, too, would have loved the rolling surf, the unending stretches of soft white sand, and the unbelievable wonder of a sun which was always on the job! All this brought an expectancy of happy things to come.

However, there was a cloud on the perpetual blue of the sky. I became quite ill. Some years earlier, I had met with an accident of a rather violent and unusual nature. One lovely day I was taking a walk near my home in the country, accompanied by a "friend"—a strong and handsome university student who was a long-standing welcome guest of the family. Quite suddenly he acted like one who was psychotically sick. Completely without provocation or warning, and giving me no time even to think, he made an apparent attempt to break my back. He picked me up and jerked my spine over a fallen tree in the way one snaps a stick of wood

in two. There being no sane or explainable reason for such
an action, it could only have been some deranged and
twisted desire to cause destruction.

Until that moment I had been blessed with an unusually
strong and perfectly fit body. After that, I had to learn to
live with pain and much spinal and internal distress. The
later advent of Murray was probably something of a miracle, but having him, as well as the loving companionship of
my husband, has more than made up for any suffering.

But now in Australia, the pressures of a new environment
and physical work which was harder than I had known in
England, combined to stir up trouble. The resulting pain
made it difficult for me to fulfill the job of caring for my
family. Doctor after doctor diagnosed and treated, bringing little relief if any. Now, at this point, our whole way of
life was to become so wonderfully changed.

We were led to a new kind of healer, a man whose simple
philosophy was different from any we had contacted before.
For many years he had practiced orthodox medicine. Then
he himself developed a deep-seated malady which his previous methods were completely unable to cure. This caused
him to ask some searching questions which finally led him
to natural rather than suppressive treatments—and with
amazingly successful results.

He represented, to us at any rate, an age-old yet new-age
type of physician. He did not advocate drugs, repressing
medicaments, or (unless imperative) surgery. Instead, he
followed as closely as possible, the healing principles used
by nature—principles which have been ruling our well-being
since time began. In his wisdom and knowledge and with
proven facts, he opened our eyes to the natural laws we
had constantly, though unwittingly, been breaking. He reminded us that the ancient meaning of the word "disease"
was "punishment by nature for disobedience of her laws,"
and that every pain, malfunction, and bodily distress was a

warning of wrongdoing. He tuned us in to his own simple faith with such thoughts as the following quotation from the *Aquarian Gospel:*

"The laws of nature are the laws of health, and he who lives according to these laws is never sick."

"Transgression of these laws is sin, and he who sins is sick."

"He who obeys the laws maintains an equilibrium in all his parts and thus ensures true harmony; and harmony is health, while discord is disease."

"Everything in nature has been made to meet the wants of man, so everything is found in medical arcanes."

Here was a mighty lot to digest at our first meeting—and yet the truth of it went home. And what in plain, everyday terms did all this entail? What must we do to regain perfect health, for none of us were as well as we might have been?

Our new treatment consisted of spinal and other manipulative treatments. It meant living entirely on the very simplest of foods and those as near to their natural source as possible. It meant avoiding all processed and refined and chemicalized products and never eating complicated combinations at one mealtime.

And it meant no meat or flesh of any kind. "You really mean," I asked our new doctor friend, "that meat is not necessary in maintaining a strong and healthy body?"

"Not only unnecessary but positively harmful," he assured me. "With the correct substitutes, you can be more vitally fit by avoiding the toxic and over-acid properties that are associated with all kinds of flesh."

What a great relief this was to me personally, for all through life I had been cajoled and badgered, against all my natural feelings, into accepting the fact that meat was essential in order to keep going at all. Now that I knew there was really no need to live on the pain of other creatures, the change was one of joy to make. In this, Ian was the real

hero and proved beyond doubt his unbigoted open-minded-
ness. He did not scorn the idea or insist that he had no
intention of giving up the things he enjoyed. But in his
usual thorough way he set about probing these theories for
himself and finding out the validity of them. He read every
book available on the subject and studied the experiences
of those who had devoted their lives to the concept of natural healing and the balance of health. He learned of the
physical make-up of man from the very beginning; of his
eating habits in every land and under all conditions; of the
worth of different foods and systems of agriculture; of the
effect on health and well-being of various types of diet.
After much deep thought he came to the conclusion that
physically, ethically, and spiritually this was the way for
us—not just for me but for all the family. As he uncovered
vital facts I tried to apply the principles to our daily lives.

We could see, for instance, the practical common sense
in the theory that that which we had come to look upon as
sickness is, in reality, nature's way of freeing an over-bur-
dened system and helping it to regain its perfect balance
and working order. If the engine of a car becomes clogged,
we do not pour in more and more oil until the inevitable
breakdown occurs; we allow the obstructing refuse to be
drained away and then replace it with clean pure oil. It is
so much the same with our bodies when they become over-
loaded and tired of the strain we put upon them. There can
be miraculous results from giving our system a digestive
rest and then taking great care about the refueling.

In other words, when we or our little ones show signs of
any pain, congestion, inflammation, or infection, then the
best possible action is to stop eating and give nature a
chance to rid the body of its refuse which is causing distress. In his book, *Faith, Love and Seaweed,* published by
Prentice-Hall, my husband deals with the scientific and
physiological aspect of this subject, so that I will be con-

cerned here only with those facts which affected my own job as wife, housekeeper, and mother. In some ways, this meant "going back to school" and re-evaluating the many false impressions and unfounded convictions that I had picked up on the way. But the rewards which followed cannot be expressed in words.

Given this fresh start, I myself became very much better. The pain was being lessened, and I felt more vitally alive in every way. Most of all, I was happy to be proving that there was no need to cause suffering in the animal world in order to keep our bodies fit. This was probably the greatest driving force behind the determination to make our plan work.

And so the stage was set for Murray's young life.

He was deeply sensitive and warmly understanding—and like every tiny child, still such a little time away from the Source of wisdom that his perceptions were clearer than ours whose insight was dulled by years of conditioning and the blindfolds of orthodoxy and habit.

We were amazed how easily and completely Murray comprehended these principles, proving again that natural insight which all children seem to be born with. One day he came out with the remark that if food was provided for man in its natural state, then it must be wrong to eat honey, which is strictly meant for the bees. Then, again, he thought entirely on his own, that milk could not be right for us either, as this was put there to feed the baby calves. Following these theories to their ultimate conclusion, he was right of course. Many strict adherents to natural living completely agree with Murray's baby reasoning. We ourselves did not follow quite so rigid a course—but convincing an inquiring four-year-old of the expediency of an occasional compromise can end in bringing a poser to oneself.

How often children act as mirrors in which we can see ourselves all too clearly, especially perhaps when they are reflecting those simple truths we have attempted to implant

Murray awaiting his call on a film set. *(Photo by Hal Conant)*

Every great champion leaves a part of himself behind—a measure of inspiration. Murray has held every world record from 200 meters to the marathon 1500-meter event. He stayed in world class for nine years and was still making world records when he was debarred, through bureaucratic confusion, from defending his titles at the Tokyo Olympics—an injustice inscribed in the Australian annals of sport for all time as "the Murray Rose Blunder." *(Photo by Bob Child, New Haven, Conn.)*

Murray receiving trophy at an international meet in Los Angeles with
Yamanaka (left) and Ishii (right), both of Japan. *(Wide World Photos)*
There are great moments in a champion's life...

...but it's hard work all
the way. *(Sydney* Morning
Herald *photo)*

2

A parent's feelings at such a moment are beyond recording. Murray on the victory dais at Rome after the 400-meter race, with Konrads (left) and Yamanaka (right). *(U.P.I. photo)*

Hero worship is the same in any language. *(Photo by Asbury Park Press, New Jersey)*

3

Young parents on a week-end walk while Murray takes it easy at home.

This was a fairy-story time.

Sailing through mine-infested seas, we and our son became acquainted once again.

4

How those in England would have loved the rolling surf, the unending stretches of soft white sand, and the unbelievable wonder of a sun that was always on the job. *(Photo by permission of the Australian Travel Association)*

The very first step Murray took was toward the water.

No toy store could ever have supplied such valuable materials or so many hours of joy.

How far-reaching are the conditions which first mold us!

The pool at our back door became our playroom, gymnasium, classroom, church, and picnic ground.

The paradise of childhood lasts such a little time—a wintertime vacation in the Australian bush.

In summer and winter we sought relaxation and exercise in strangely remote places in the Australian bush.

within them! Murray, for instance, was brought up to accept man's responsibility to be both a friend and a protector of animals. Now it so happened that my mother had given me a fur coat before I left England, and the fact that I had kept it around somewhat discredited my sincerity. One cold night as I was leaving to attend a party, I thoughtlessly put it over my shoulders and went into Murray's nursery to say good-night. Instead of throwing his arms around my neck, he drew back at the unexpected sight and feel of fur. Since then, I can never think of the wearing of furs without also thinking of the untamed savage which is still so much a part of us. Fortunately there is now a rich range of substitute fabrics which beautifully enhances the truly feminine and brings individuality to the wearer.

Having a delicate father, Murray was somewhat handicapped even before he came into the world, and perhaps this was not the background one would expect a world champion to spring from. And yet it could have been the impetus that brought extra striving—the very condition necessary to work for something better.

Strangely enough, successful people frequently have their beginnings in some obstacle to overcome. It creates a need, a challenge to do something about it. As we are constantly remaking ourselves into our own image, we *can* turn it into something wonderfully rewarding.

One of many such examples is that of the great Finnish athlete Paavo Nurmi, who was born with unusually weak legs. Desiring to strengthen them, he took up running. Such determination and belief did he show that Nurmi broke world records at the Olympic Games.

Much strengthened by belief in these theories, and encouraged by our own immediate good results, we made up our minds to try and undo any harm that had been set in motion and to put health and happiness in its place. Through our mistakes, lack of knowledge, and sometimes even laziness, we are often responsible for much of our children's suffering. Children themselves have a natural wisdom unclouded by years of confusing impressions.

A friend who had once attended a lecture given by the great Albert Einstein passed on a reminder of the size of the job we parents have been entrusted to fulfill. He told us how he had listened intently to the words of this genius, finding the profound theories of relativity a little beyond him at times. Afterwards he asked him if there was some way of helping a layman such as himself to comprehend more clearly.

"You know what an acorn is?" answered Einstein. "Well, if you pick up an acorn and put it in the palm of your hand, you are then holding in that tiny space the whole of a large and wonderfully beautiful oak tree!"

Now I never pick up a newly born infant without remembering this simple yet stupendous thought and envision the mighty potential, the unknown talent and the joy of living, all locked inside and waiting to unfold. What a dreadful tragedy if it should be stultified through ignorance and lack of wise attention! It is not enough to merely conform to the patterns set by the "authorities" of the day, to believe without question every high-sounding theory and become zombies with conditioned minds. The wisest guidance speaks through our inborn instinct, which is eternally counseling us, if we will only stop to listen.

Would you teach your child to walk with a limp? Or to look at things with one eye closed? Are these thoughts so absurd? How few of us have been shown the way to a quietly integrated mind, unobstructed insight, and a perfectly healthy body! As our doctor teacher opened our eyes to the infallible workings of nature and we relied more and more on her unerring laws, we became convinced that here was the only way to restore perfect health and attain full potential.

When we changed an old habit or attempted a new form of treatment we always explained to Murray the reasons for our action. Baby as he was, he co-operated with understanding and was more than willing to do his share. Children are like that. When given sincere and honest reasons they seem to have an uncanny way of perceiving the truth of things far more easily perhaps than we—and they *want* to go along with it. We dare not jeopardize their right to a free, full and perfectly healthy life.

It is being more and more understood that thoughts can change the whole chemistry of our bodies for good or ill, so that the attitude of everyone—especially the mother—has a tremendous effect on the health as well as the happiness of a home. The wholehearted adoption of psychosomatic medicine is a further proof of the interrelationship of mind and body. Just a moment's reflection will substantiate that.

On receiving some unexpected and disturbing news a person will turn pale and begin to tremble. In a highly nervous state of mind, we lose all desire for food. When deeply depressed, our steps become heavy and our movements slower. Embarrassment or guilt brings a flush to the skin, while great grief has turned the hair white and even upset the balance of the brain. And there are authenticated cases of babies being poisoned by a mother giving vent to anger while feeding them. One could go on and on, but the point has been made that the body definitely reacts to the mental processes.

It is up to us then to see that those pictures are happy, healthy and safe ones. Children especially are most receptive to the thoughts of the grownups around them. I know one mother—and I'm sure we all know at least one of her prototypes—who was constantly on edge with anxiety whenever her child was out of sight. Consequently the child invariably came home crying because of some hurt, or pale with an oncoming sickness. That which we fear, we seem to draw to us. Happily the reverse is also true. How sad then to reflect on the negative attitude taken by modern medicine!

Talk to any medical student, and you will find that, in general, his instruction is not so much based on the ways of preserving health and following the simple laws of nature as much as combating "inevitable" disease, illness, and unbalanced conditions. Seemingly his professors accept the belief that pain and sickness are part of the natural and normal heritage of man. Isn't it possible—and even probable—that all this emphasis on disease and abnormality is keeping our hospitals crowded by counteracting the all-wise healing hand of nature? Somewhere along the line we must have gone off course. This is man's and not God's way of thinking.

There are times, of course, when medical science may offer the only way out, especially in cases of accident. But the skilled doctor will also possess the qualities that enable him to serve as a guide to better health. When his patient recovers, the dedicated physician urges that sound living practices and positive thinking be substituted for those practices which encourage disease, so that a higher standard of health can be reached.

We were set in motion by an All-Knowing, All-Providing Mind, whose law is Supreme Harmony. By succumbing to fear and other emotions, instead of seeking wisdom in the quiet stillness of our hearts, we upset the perfect rhythm of our bodies and so bring about illness or suffering.

Has there ever been greater proof of such an apparent miracle than that shown by Elizabeth Barrett? Brought up in the belief that she was too delicate to live a normal life, and completely dominated by the wrong thinking of a tyrant father, she was freed from her prison, her whole body revitalized, and her life transformed by the joy and strength that came through the love of Robert Browning. She lived to experience a full and happy life, and her thoughts and gratitude live on in the beauty of her poetry.

As our whole being is renewed and recharged all the time, we can bring such wonderfully improved conditions by consciously believing in health and happiness. Every cell immediately responds. Only the violation of Divine Principles can bring distress, for no power on earth can upset the perfect balance of the natural law. I see it as a sort of Universal Scales where every action and thought, no matter how big or how small, is weighed and given back to us in some form. Greed and lack of discipline causes imbalance; then pain and inharmonious conditions will eventually follow. Thoughts of jealousy, envy, and hate make an ugly impression on the most beautiful features, while constant joy and compassion bring a warm loveliness all of their own.

The tremendous influence we ourselves have upon our own lives is vividly illustrated by the life of Madame Schumann-Heink. When young, she longed to be a singer, but among many other obstacles she was told repeatedly that she was far too plain ever to be successful before the public and was advised to take up sewing instead. Even so, she clung to her belief and continued to develop and express such beauty through her voice that the world came to hear and admire her.

We found that Murray never tired of hearing stories built around such thoughts. He soon found for himself that God was not some far-distant overlord who doles out pleasure and pain at will but a wonderfully benevolent friend whose loving power is seen and felt everywhere, in the beauty of the flowers, in the faith and trust of a pet, and most of all in his own heart; a Father, even of fathers, who wants only to lead us to happiness and who gave us all we have in order to express His loving thoughts. When we try to use our body and mind to do this work, He, too, will be working with us so that we cannot fail.

This is not only the truest but also the most infallible way to help a child grow from within and, through self-discipline and self-seeking, to be his own guide and teacher —essential attributes to those youngsters reaching for high goals.

Our own guidance, strength, and help came through a greater understanding of these eternal Universal Principles. Here lies all a parent needs in the way of philosophy, psychology, and the wisdom of truths which can never change.

In the basic law of Cause and Effect we found the answer to most of our problems, and the means by which they might be solved. Most things which seemingly go wrong we so often bring upon ourselves. There is nothing we cannot attain in body or mind by simply sticking to the rules, by going along with the Cosmic forces and not trying to pit our own puny strength against them.

Such a philosophy makes those difficult periods of "illness" far easier to handle. By giving the digestive system a rest, and then introducing only the purest and simplest of foods, the body is stimulated into helping nature clear away any accumulated impurities, this being the whole purpose of that which we call sickness.

The great difference in treating the natural way is that no drugs or harsh medicine are allowed to repress the natural forces and so prevent the body from throwing off toxic material. When the bloodstream has become as clean and healthy as it was intended to be, no germs can thrive there. This was the long and difficult task we set out to accomplish and it tested our belief and patience many, many times. However, we came to trust the superior medical skills of nature and tried to help on the good results rather than hinder them.

We were shown how so-called ailments are really healing crises and that by providing rest, warmth, hot and cold compresses, internal enemas, and most of all by temporarily suspending the extra work of digesting and eliminating further foods, we can do much to assist the healing work.

As Murray was fed on pure, natural foods his body became fitter, which also meant that it began using its energies to throw off waste material it didn't need. We went through a number of these "spring cleanings" as a result of Murray's early imperfect diet as well as the poisonous vaccine which we had mistakenly sanctioned.

At first, these upsets took the form of feverish colds or influenza. Then followed whooping cough and measles. But the name given to a disease is unimportant in itself. Each is a manifestation used by nature in her wise attempt to purify the system.

These periods are a real challenge to one's belief, but it is amazing how naturally and easily a child will accept all you do without fuss, fret, or complaint. Anyway, that was our experience. When a high temperature is present and one is lying in bed, there is no desire for food, and the mind soon accustoms itself to the idea of drinking only—either water or water flavored with a little lemon. There are usually long periods of sleep or half-sleep but during the waking hours one can always be on hand to make everything as happy as possible.

At these times you will find that hot and cold packs get the pores working overtime in ridding the body of poisons and give a feeling of relaxation, as well as making the little one know that you are working *with* him to make him well again. Once again, the finest medicine is a happy and positive atmosphere. As assurance and joy are being absorbed, their wonderful influence is quickly on the job of healing from within. When the child is made to realize that troublemaking toxins are being cleared away and that this will help him to feel fitter in a very short time, it encourages his happy co-operation.

As the fever subsides, diluted juices may be given. Pineapple juice with its quality for cleansing and its natural sugar, we found to be excellent.

Now there will be a need for favorite stories, games, and fun. It is essentially a time when the power of love works its own magic.

Massage can be helpful in several ways and is soothing and enjoyable to the patient. Make sure the body is kept warm, using a sun lamp or heater if necessary, then massage limbs and spine, working around but not on the vertebrae. This will help to disperse any poisons which may have collected there and will keep muscles toned. A relaxing massage on nerve centers is valuable in easing tension and inducing sleep when congestion, fever, or coughing causes distress and wakefulness.

As Murray became a young athlete, this early practice of massage proved to be quite a boon. It often helped him to relax before big races and braced up the muscles to keep them in top swimming order. Once a habit is formed very early, with sympathy and understanding, it goes on paying off. Even when the strain was at its greatest, and the whole world waited to see what Murray could do, even then the old routine would work. Tension could be taken away for a while and the body relaxed into valuable, strength-giving rest.

The next stage of our "healing crisis" would be a few days on an all-fruit diet. That is reached when the temperature is normal and the tongue is clean. If grapes are in season, their abundant natural sugar makes them an excellent tonic. But any ripe, juicy fruit is beneficial and staying with one type at a time is the wisest plan.

If the weather is sunny, now is the time to take rugs and cushions out of doors and let the sunshine take over for a while. I remember those "getting better" hours of playing dominoes or snakes and ladders. If I had to be busy in the house, I would find boxes and tins to be painted, or any other interesting job, so long as the youngster was kept occupied and contented. The object of one such project is still in use in our home. It is a stoutly made toy box built from fruit crates and then brightly painted. Having survived a sea voyage across the world, as well as a quarter of a century of battering, it serves the useful purpose of hiding sundry household gadgets—as good an excuse as any to preserve a boxful of memories.

To quickly gain strength and replace any lack of minerals or vitamins, vegetable juices are excellent. And in order to make them more palatable and tempting I sometimes warmed them and added brewer's yeast for its extra content of the B vitamins. Another easily digested and nutritive drink which I found most helpful was made by straining off the liquid after whole wheat had been simmered for a time. With a little honey, this is pleasant and nourishing. As the appetite returns, a vegetable salad or carefully cooked vegetables can be given, then a little protein, and finally the more concentrated carbohydrate foods.

Thus over a period of years, by following this regime, we gradually got rid of much that was causing Murray to be ill, and his body was built anew with the goodness of natural foods. It is quite amazing how quickly one becomes accustomed to this form of treatment, especially after knowing that vitally fit feeling which follows when much dead and poisonous material has been eliminated. No longer does illness hold its dread. There are no more anxious waits for the doctor to call. Gone is the nightmare of operations to remove organs from a little body, which at one time we had believed might be necessary. A certain amount of basic physiological knowledge is all that is necessary so that a mother truly understands what she should do and why.

Probably the very first lesson is never to worry about a

child losing weight during these "clean-outs." What is weight anyway? Very often it is merely unhealthy waste tissue. In no time at all he will build up fine new healthy cells and be stronger than ever. Fresh air and exercise will finish off the job.

The thing that made our task worthwhile was that from a baby on, Murray did *everything that was asked of him.* We have thought, studied, and tried to help where we could, but only his own courage, belief, self-discipline, and tireless determination made Murray's success possible.

## CHAPTER 5

# A WATER BABY FINDS HIS OWN ELEMENT

There was soft white sand at our harbor pool, shady trees, grass and flowers, and, with great good fortune, a shark net all around. In those days few people ever came there. It was indeed a perfect setting for a little one to grow in, and for a mother to learn *her* job of helping.

This beach was to become our playroom, gymnasium, classroom, church, and picnic ground. Here Murray would play and exercise free as the air. Here it was that he learned to swim. At first he was uncertain of the water, as most babies are, but as we wanted him strong and without fears, I set about getting over this first hurdle.

Each day I would dig a large, deep hole in the sand near enough to the edge of the sea for it to fill with water as the tide rolled in. In this hole, Murray felt safe, and at the same time got the feeling and love of that which was to become his natural element.

Gradually, I led him from this little pool into the big harbor pool where, with his hand in mine, he was soon swimming and loving it. After a while, I would take away my support and let him go on his own. Wherever I swam he followed. Each day we made a longer swim until he was more confident in the water than on land. Many years before and in much the same way, my own father had taken me away out to sea, there being no sharks to fear on the English coast, and taught me to dog-paddle back on my own.

In his bath every night Murray played a game of breathing above the water and blowing it out underneath. So, without realizing it, he began to learn the correct breathing for swimming which is so difficult for a tiny child to master at first.

Our hard work was almost ruined by the usual sadistic young bully who seems to get onto every beach. One day I was watching Murray's fair head bobbing along in the sea when, to my horror, it disappeared. Then I realized he was being held under. The seconds ticked away to a frightening length of time until, fully clothed, I had to wade out and bring him to the surface, exhausted and terrified. The life guard arrived and taught the guilty young hooligan the lesson of his life. As a result of this experience Murray lost all confidence, and though we managed to coax him back into the water, it was a long, long time before his fears could be erased.

Highly imaginative, as most little ones are, he developed a nightmare dread of going under water. For him, some eerie fantasy seemed to be lurking there now. This caused a serious setback to his preparation, and restoration of his faith and love of swimming became a real challenge. Naturally, the biggest hurdle was in getting him to dive. In fact, it took about two years of gently taking one step at a time, day after day, going with him under the water, proving again and again that there was nothing there to be afraid of, until at last this bogey was dead.

Even then, Murray might not have learned to dive so soon but for a valuable tip passed on by an old-timer. "Get the child to imagine there's a wooden hoop in the air, between him and the water, which he must dive over on his way in," he suggested, "and just see the difference!" The result was amazing, for this simple illusion produced a natural spring and caused the body to shape and move into the correct diving position. From this time on, Murray dived beautifully and with complete confidence.

During those first baby days spent at the pool Murray quickly made friends with the groundsmen there. As they cleaned up the sands and worked in the garden, he loved to be shown how to do little jobs. Whenever I had some work to do or a trip to make to the local store I could safely depend on their attentive care. I well remember on one such occasion the surprising little scene which greeted my return. As I came to the top of the long flight of steps leading down to the beach where a new path was under construction, I could see a ring of those husky workmen standing around my tiny son. Naturally wondering what it was all about, I approached near enough to hear Murray solemnly telling the story of Goldilocks to his absorbed and encouraging audience. Who could have helped a feeling of gratitude for their big and friendly hearts as they shared a child's bright world of make-believe!

Another event which seemed to illustrate either a natural stoicism, or a small mind confused as to right and wrong, also occurred on the beach when Murray was around four years old. As usual during the winter months, he had been pretty much alone except for his workmen friends. Evidently the men had been "burning off," and as the bonfire died down, Murray (so he told me later) had put his hand right into the glowing embers, probably to pick out some object which attracted him. It was not until we arrived home some hours later that I opened his tightly clenched fist and saw that his hand was quite severely burned. He must have been in very great pain—and unaccountably had told no one.

I was greatly disturbed that my sympathetic understanding had been doubted and to be so clearly shown how unpredictable a grownup's reactions can seem to a little one.

## Shadows in the Sun

Now and then, as we swam in our harbor pool, we would
see a battleship slowly pass by on her way into port—
marked and pitted from the shell fire of a recent enemy
entanglement. A day or so later, we might find in our mail-
box a gold-lettered card, "With the Captain's Compliments . . ." We were invited to attend a dance given by
the officers of HMS ——. Across the back of the invitation
were instructions to guests that searchlights, being played
from the ship, would be a signal that the dance was off
and she was recalled into action.

As we walked up the carpeted gangway we would be
greeted by a salute in gallant naval fashion. We were the
ones who should have been doing the saluting, as in our
hearts we did many times during these dreamlike floating
galas. Not even pantomime showmanship could have competed with the magical change of scene brought about overnight by these war-weary sailors. Every inch of the vessel
would gleam with fresh paint; grim stains were surrepti-
tiously scrubbed away and guns hidden by flags and bunt-
ing. But still there were places where no amount of paint
and camouflage could hide the obvious marks of a recent
fight, and the glitter and laughter seemed so thin a veil
over yesterday—and tomorrow.

Murray liked to hear all about these shipboard occasions,
but it was a puzzling world to live in, where men killed each
other one day and gaily danced the next; this was something he was yet too young to comprehend. Naturally he
enjoyed the visits of these navy men to our home and loved
to share their fun in the curling Bondi breakers as they
swept us into shore. One day before dinner Murray was
chatting to two such youngsters, fresh from sea battles and

wakeful nights, when their eyes started to close. Could they rest a little before dinnertime, they asked. One in the guest room, and the other on Murray's bed, they completely passed out for twenty-four hours, while Murray spent the night on the living room sofa. This was a rare occasion when we could provide the one thing they needed—peace.

Anything in the water, or on it, has naturally appealed to Murray. And our son's joy was complete when he was allowed to toddle round the deck of a destroyer with one of his gold-braided hero friends and was briefed in the mechanics of releasing a depth-charge or shown the planes being signaled into place on the wide decks of their mother aircraft carrier, though at that time he little understood the lethal reasons for such activities.

He knew how it felt to be confined in a submarine and chatted excitedly in the private quarters of his seafaring hosts, as he shared their man-sized hunks of bread and jam, served by a jaunty cockney sailor.

Then came the happy night when there was every reason for gaiety as we boarded the flagship which had just returned from the signing of peace with Japan. She was radiant with lights and laden with flowers. "There are no fewer than six admirals aboard tonight," said my white-uniformed partner as we kept in step to "Rum and Coca-Cola." Champagne flowed. A fountain played on the main deck while the quacking of ducks paddling round it brought back a nostalgic note of English village ponds.

## No Barriers in Sport

Mindful today of the friendship which later sprang up between Murray and his 1956 Olympic opponent, the great Japanese champion Yamanaka, some incidents during these wartime days take on a new significance and interest.

For instance, when Murray was about four years old he appeared in an advertisement boosting Australian morale and appealing for savings to be invested in War Bonds. The picture showed him sailing a toy yacht and looking out to sea. The headline read: "WILL THE JAPS COME HERE IN THEIR BIG SHIPS, DADDY?"

One evening, at about this time, I was walking alone along the harbor's edge when I paused to take in the sunset scene, which usually brought such a feeling of peace. But on this occasion, I had an uncanny sense of something being wrong. There was an eerie stillness which brought apprehension and fear. I looked into the darkening waters and became strangely aware of several pairs of slanting eyes looking back at me. So vivid and alarming was this presentiment that I almost ran to the nearby cafe, glad to be within the warm presence of Ian and Murray, who awaited me there. Later, I told Ian of the incident. I don't think either of us was really surprised when we heard next day that three midget Japanese submarines had slipped into Sydney harbor that night, penetrating the anti-submarine net in order to attempt the destruction of Allied shipping.

Though one American troopship received some damage the enemy subs were sighted before great harm was done. Depth charges brought the inevitable end which the suicide crews must have known would be theirs. I thought of those men as they silently waited just a few yards away from where I had stood. Little wonder the air had been so charged with fear and the hopelessness of impending death.

Only a week later, I had a similar feeling of some fearful presence. Several times I checked the windows and doors around our apartment. I could not relax and go to sleep. When the sirens sounded (the first time in Sydney and, happily, the last), I knew that that was what I had been waiting for. The ensuing bombardment from a Japanese vessel sent shells screaming over our roof and crashing into the other side of the harbor.

It is possible to feel only great sadness that fear and intense nationalism can so blind man to love of man. Since those days Murray has become acquainted with the true spirit of Japan and its people. He has enjoyed the beauty of their country and the warmth of their hospitality. Above all, he has shared the Olympic camaraderie with their great champions and, to me personally, the press photographs of two smiling young Olympians with hands clasped in friendship will forever be superimposed across any grim scenes of battle.

## And So the Twig Is Bent

When it comes to youngsters' questions, what a store of knowledge we need in answering them at times! How tantalizing, difficult, and even profound they can be with their simple trust and that wisdom we glimpse that is often nearer the truth than our own!

We were often caught unprepared. For instance, every one of us is given this poser if we've brought the usual ideas of Christmas into our home: "Is there really a Father Christmas?" I remember I had just exploded the theory of the fairy who exchanged silver sixpences for lost teeth when Murray intelligently followed up this thought with the direct question about our Christmas myth.

This question is quite a problem, for we can cause much harm by giving a child the idea that we are not to be trusted. And what joy could be taken away without that Christmas spirit of giving!

"That depends on what we mean by 'real,'" I said slowly, giving myself time to think. "Long, long ago there lived in Germany a great saint called Nicholas. He taught how wonderful it was to give—especially to those who are without. The teachings of this saint are remembered at Christmastime when his spirit lives through all people, especially perhaps through parents, who want to pass on his message of kindness and good will. It is a season of giving— giving whatever you have. And children can give even more than grownups for their love and help is the greatest gift of all.

"As our Christmas is a time when we remember the birthday of Christ we have an extra reason for expressing our gratitude. What could be a better way than by bringing happiness to everyone, including our most dear ones? We call this idea 'Father Christmas,' but you can see that it is really the spirit of love that parents are trying to bring to their children. So Christmas Day is a day set aside when we remember how we should live every other day too."

Murray seemed quite happy about this explanation. Christmas never lost any of its joy for us, though perhaps the great thrill of the unknown was rather taken away.

The answer to such questions is of vital importance to a little one's mind, and the way we handle them can have far-reaching effects. They can be opportunities for us to start building tender constructive thoughts—but on the other hand, careless explanations may well create confusion and doubt which can take years to remove.

Here is another situation we all have to meet:

"Why is that pussy so still in the road?" I was walking to the beach with Murray one day and knew that another first impression was needing a careful answer, for the thought of death had come into his baby mind.

Again and again I found that an understanding of metaphysics made these delicate tasks so much more natural and happy in their effects. "That's only pussy's old coat that he has left behind. The real pussy, the one that God made, has gone to join all the others in heaven. One day he will have a lovely new coat and will come back here again. It is rather like you taking off your clothes and going to sleep, then waking in the morning, putting a new suit on and going out to have another happy day." Children accept these simple explanations and do not build morbid thoughts.

We didn't take Murray to regular church services when he was small, but quite spontaneously he sometimes led me into a church where he loved to sit awhile as though learning from the beauty and wisdom of thoughts that had been left there. This lifting experience we tried to carry home and renew each evening.

"Time for 'lax" was Murray's expression for the quiet period before bed in pre-school days. We would sit, relaxed, in front of a fire and chat about things we had done and seen during the day and maybe answer questions and smooth away troubles, finishing with a few words to our Loving Father/Friend and a little song or hymn. I often wish a family could keep up the warm moments of confidence and straightening out which take place when children are very young. How much calmer our sleep! How many hurts and worries we could avoid!

To keep me reminded of these thoughts I have a tiny china choirboy standing on my shelf, bought as a gift with the first babyhood pennies. We used to light his candle during those quiet evening talks. The shelf where he lives is now gay with little people who have joined him, one by one, through the years.

From colorful places and in odd situations Murray has remembered my love of small dolls and greatly added to the collection. There's a coy nineteenth-century Parisienne whom he brought back from France after the Rome Olympics . . . a sari-draped beauty from an Indian temple . . . and a veil dancer he found in a Bahrein market when the Olympic team were forced to land there and were grounded all night in the desert heat. There's a Maori in ceremonial dress who came back from New Zealand and his first overseas tour. From championships in Tokyo he bought a geisha girl—and a tangoing Señorita from Mexico. The one most cherished, though of smallest value, is still the little choirboy, but each and every one has its own built-in story of drama and poignant memory.

All who have changed countries will understand how hard it can be to find yourself in strange surroundings—perhaps not quite fitting into a different way of thinking and behaving—often very lonely and feeling a heartache for familiar ways and scenes. No matter how much kindness is shown by those around you, there is always a certain conditioning by lifelong experience that is not easy to forget.

We were grateful to Australia and the benefits she gave to us. Living in so gay and sunny an atmosphere one could never be sad for long. Murray was completely happy with his life and friends, for he remembered nothing else. In our thoughts, however, there was a continual tug-of-war which was never permanently resolved. The soft beauty of England and her gentle ways were poignantly reviewed from time to time, so that Murray must have felt that he belonged in two places. Quite naturally, Sydney became his first love and true home.

About the time Murray was five, a young swimming trainer came to our beach. His name was familiar as he had been a local champion and well-known for his pluck and fighting spirit. (This spirit has since helped us through many a dark moment!) Wanting to ensure a correct style, we handed our young son over for proper training. What a deep, lifelong tie was started that day . . . the day Sam Herford first began to show Murray how to kick, and pull with his arms!

As it happened, we had previously had a rather unfor-

tunate experience, for Murray had started tuition from
another instructor before Sam took over; but somehow this
man must have lacked understanding. Murray was fearful
of his lessons and frequently came home sobbing, saying
that when he attempted to dive, the coach had sneered
that he looked "like a bag of potatoes falling into the water."
Remembering the effort he always made and the necessity
to rebuild his full confidence, so unperceptive an attitude
brought home the great need to really know the nature of
those who teach our young ones.

In the years ahead, Sam was to give his time, thought,
sleep, and very heart to Murray.

## Classroom without Walls

At first our only thought was to have him confident and
happy in the water. We knew that swimming was the perfect exercise for building a strong and well-proportioned
body, and that fresh air, sunshine, and water was a pretty
good mixture for making any child fit. But it wasn't very
long before it became apparent that something above average was emerging from these two.

The perfect rhythm and grace of movement were a delight to see and most unusual, we were told, in one so
young. Sam knew how to teach the technique of classic
stroking. Murray, always earnest and trying his hardest to
learn, seemed to find natural self-expression in the element
he most loved.

During the beginning stages we would place cushions
on a stool so that Murray could lie face downward, with
his arms, legs, and head free to move. In this way he was
able to practice the correct movements and co-ordination
of swimming strokes.

If you feel youth is slipping away, or you're not in the

shape you used to be, try training with a youngster and sticking to the rules you make for him. It brings the exhilaration of living all over again. There are parents who will tell you, though I doubt that they mean it, that the best years of their lives have been given to their children. We found the very reverse to be true. It took a child to give *us* the best time of our life and add richly to its meaning too.

Every morning before breakfast we started the day on the beach—exercising, running, and swimming together. We found that the habit of practicing deep rhythmic breathing was especially helpful, not only for its value in developing lung capacity but also for its over-all calming and co-ordinating effect.

This habit is of tremendous help during periods of excitement and stress for it encourages control and relaxation as well as attuning the body to perfect rhythmic movement.

Through summer and winter, in rain and cold, that early rendezvous with the morning was rarely missed from the time of Murray's babyhood right up to the Melbourne Olympics. Sharing this "in-touchness" with the elements and nature, the family seemed wonderfully close, and I often wished that the essence of those moments might be preserved and materialize into something beautiful and lasting.

Murray was still only pre-kindergarten age, but his days were filled for all that. In addition to his other activities, lessons were now added. If every child could have such a classroom! On the firm deep sand, and with a stick, he learned his letters and numbers. He was soon spelling well and writing sentences, as well as mastering the rudiments of arithmetic with the aid of boxes and pebbles. We talked of other countries and a great deal about nature, flowers, and animals. And of how God is everywhere—His strength and love in the water, the sunshine, and the air—making everything fun and little bodies fit.

As for self-expression, there was no end to the source of creative materials to be found. Strangely shaped driftwood, seaweed, grasses, sea-smooth pebbles of every hue, and shells lined with silver and pearl. Most of all, there was the sand itself, always available to be molded into any image. How many mansions, native villages, forests, and fairy castles were built—and mentally lived in—it would be impossible to recall! I only know that the most famous of toy stores could never have supplied such valuable material nor so many hours of joy. One thing is certain, there was never a place for any toys or "fun" suggestive of violence or destruction of life.

We made a practice of first reading stories and frequently changing the material before retelling them to our tiny son. Much of my own childhood fear and highly nervous reactions had been due, in part at least, to unsupervised reading matter when I was no doubt too young to digest it. A certain maid, for instance, delighted in telling terrifying tales and revealing facts without beauty or sensitivity to cushion them.

When it came to raising a child of our own, the gradual unfolding of knowledge seemed of paramount concern. First impressions, we knew, grooved a pattern for future thinking and approach to life. Early emotional shocks are difficult to erase.

The television monster was yet to be born and one we were not challenged to deal with. However, the father of young children was telling us recently how the television set at his home had broken down, and how for six peaceful weeks he had delayed its repair. During that time, he confessed, the family had enjoyed some of the happiest and warmest evenings of their lives. They played games, found time and quiet for the uninterrupted exchange of views, and came closer together than ever before.

I often think that children brought up before this age of sophisticated toys and highly perfected models had a great advantage. The desire to create and the need for ingenuity in forming things for themselves is ninety per cent of the pleasure and satisfaction derived from play.

I can remember a number of times when something, such as the playbox, was just thought up to fill a need for occupation, but turned out to be a truly useful object. Sometimes even a real quality of beauty evolved.

For instance, there was the unforgettable cathedral—a model which grew out of blocks of wood, cardboard and paint and sundry household scraps. One day during a "getting well" period Murray started building, occasionally asking for help and materials, and the shape of a church began to appear. Somehow it kept growing; each day some new idea was added until it was transformed into a truly lovely cathedral. We put on a roof, painted biblical scenes on pieces of glass which were set in as windows. Inside we built an altar and embroidered a scrap of material with golden thread to go on it.

Then came tiny candlesticks made from wire and silver paper, which held the smallest white birthday-cake candles; and minute perfume bottles as vases for the real flowers. We bought tiny figures and dressed them up as clergy and congregation. Finally, a whole wedding party arrived, the bride, groom, bridesmaids, and all. Next we rolled out the inevitable red carpet. Then the waiting cars were placed at the entrance and gradually the whole neat cathedral square took shape. This became such a place of wonder and joy that we just left it there. Many friends, both young and old, often came to take a look, especially at night when we made the room dark and lit the candles. So real was the flow of light coming through the stained glass windows, so warmly alive were the wee figures standing in ceremonial fashion, that we would not have been in the least surprised had some magic produced the strains of a wedding march.

How long it stood there, I can't remember now, but for almost two years, I believe, while for all that time the room it occupied was pretty much out of action, to say nothing of the intricate cleaning problem it brought. But there it stayed, constantly cared for and added to, and the means of building far more than a model made from odds and ends.

We like to think that *we* are doing the teaching—poor, ignorant parents! But what of the lessons we ourselves are learning all over again? Those fast-fading lessons of truth, beauty, and joy in simple things: true wisdom which we sometimes fail to grasp even after a lifetime of the profoundest study. This time of caring for little ones is also a time when, all too often, we mothers become enmeshed in the day-to-day routine of many extra jobs and do not value the treasure which is ours until too late to call it back. Perhaps this is just another of the many gems that wise old prophet had in mind when he said:

> Every one hath got rubies in his bundle,
> But how to open the knot
> He doth not know,
> And therefore is he a pauper.

This paradise of childhood lasts such a little time, a paradise we parents are most privileged to share. And yet how easy to confuse our values during these busy days, to fret and fuss and fill our minds with passing trivialities.

Perhaps we cut short a walk or game in our housewifely zeal to clean tiny footmarks from the floor, forgetting that all too soon those small running feet will be man-sized and perhaps walking on floors many miles away. A crease in a party dress is allowed to cause angry words, when that childish hug would be worth a thousand dresses after our youngster is grown and gone from home. When our loving attention is needed to tell a story we may turn that attention to chatting of inconsequences on the phone. Or we just can't tear ourselves away from a favorite newspaper column or an intriguing soap opera on TV. Time-wasters that add almost nothing to our happiness can insidiously steal away a storehouse of gems in the form of tender hours and the creating of a bond that can last long after baby days are over.

## Being "Broken In"

Schooldays caught up with us all too soon, and the wearing of constricting clothes was perhaps the hardest change for Murray to make. He had known only freedom up to this time. Even on rare visits to the city he never wore more than simple white shorts. Today numbers of people have the same ideas, but even those few years ago, the reactions were quite amazing. We would be stopped by interfering old ladies who admonished me for my lack of decorum: "You should be ashamed to take out a child 'half-clothed!'" At the same time others would enthusiastically declare: "That's my idea of how a child *should* be dressed!"

In fact, as a result of this constant exposure to sunshine, sea, and air, Murray, with his brown body and very fair hair, came to be known as "the little golden boy of Redleaf Beach." It is perhaps no coincidence that today he owns a gold medal giving him the lifelong freedom of this very beach.

This idyll ended with the advent of school, for conventions of the civilized world had to be learned.

At this stage when our small ones show signs of becoming individuals, how dear are their first spontaneous gestures of thought. The little gift or card, proudly purchased with hard-to-save pennies and shyly brought home to cheer us when we are sick. One precious flower, or perhaps a whole sweet bunch of them, gathered on the way back from school, and held out in that eager, expectant way children have when they know full well they have touched our softest spot. Such offerings are surely heaven-blessed.

Murray's regime continued in much the same way before and after school, and it wasn't very long after starting at kindergarten that Murray had his first taste of racing before a crowd in the big Olympic Pool. Special permission was requested for him to swim for the main school in an interschool contest.

After the first groundwork has been put in, competition is a wonderful stimulus, and at this point, probably more than at any other, the influence of parents can turn the tide. When our young ones are still looking to us to show the way, encouragement, understanding, and enthusiastic help can change the whole course of events.

We let Murray join a club at the world-famous Bondi Beach and found that the week between Saturday morning races was just long enough to keep him keen and hold his interest to train. He knew we understood how hard he tried and how proud we were to see him succeed. A parent soon discovers that success grows out of praise, thanksgiving, and constructive thoughts. And that condemnation of any sort is disheartening and destructive.

The joy and fun of being with so many others who shared his sport and the experience of having to overcome nervousness and to perform in public was invaluable. Very quickly he began breaking records in his own age group.

Those who give their time and thought to running these clubs are doing a great job in helping to build character and sportsmanship into our future men and women. Ten years after Murray joined the Bondi Club, three of its boys were to represent their country in the 1956 Olympic Games, and all three were to be in the final of the great marathon mile of swimming. So, in effect, they were racing in a world series every Saturday morning. This was a tremendous stimulus to determined effort and a builder of courage and fighting spirit.

Before giving everything to swimming, Murray tried many other sports. His first reaction to the riding lessons which he took every week was one I have heard from many small children: "Why do we have to put a bit in a horse's mouth, or whip him to make him carry us?" Bareback riding would have seemed much more acceptable.

Later, when every spare minute had to be devoted to his swimming and training, riding was one sport he didn't really mind giving up. As he became a star, one by one all other sporting interests had to be laid aside. He always enjoyed and played a good game of tennis, but Murray's coach could not encourage this. The muscular development which comes through constant use of a racket is antipathetic to the relaxation necessary for those powerful, rhythmic laps that win close races in a swimming pool. Rowing, a favorite summer sport in Murray's school, was also out because it made muscles stiff and taut instead of assuring a fluid, relaxed movement so necessary for prowess in the water. There was nothing he liked better than taking his place as lock forward in a tough game of rugby union. "I hope I don't have to give up football," he would say. But eventually athletic coaches advised him not to risk serious damage to a limb. "I have seen too many great potentials ruined by a torn muscle and broken bones," Professor Frank Cotton of Sydney University told him, "you'll have all the exercise and fun you can use in swimming, my boy."

Although I understood and deeply sympathized with Murray's hard and painful decision, it was not until years later that I realized the full measure of sacrifice that giving up rugby football had entailed. Not, in fact, until the time of the Rome Olympics in 1960. An old school friend of Murray's was the son of one of the ambassadors in Rome. While this young man was kindly driving me around that city in search of an electric juicing machine to make the pints of carrot juice needed, he told me just how much this had really meant to our young champion son.

"It is the dream of every boy to make the first football team you know," he said to me almost reproachfully. "How few boys are ever called upon for the sacrifice Murray was asked to make. It must have hurt a lot—perhaps only we boys knew how much. I have never forgotten how quietly and uncomplainingly he accepted his loss." Certainly Murray had never worried us by showing how deeply upset he was at the time.

The advice had been well meant, I know, but just how right, or wrong, it was I have no way of knowing. And I am very sure that Murray realized there was far more to gain through a medium that could lead to the heights. In thinking back, I naturally feel a sadness and regret at so much pleasure having to be taken away. We sincerely believed (and I trust rightly so) that any activity, whether in sport or social life that seemingly impinged on his attaining his final goal could have destroyed a greater happiness and sense of fulfillment. No wonder King Solomon deemed wisdom the greatest of gifts. He must have been a parent too.

Murray was finding out the hard and often painful lesson, as all athletes must, that those whose goal is set on reaching the top in any chosen sport must be dedicated to that sport alone, for the demands and standards of today necessitate that all other interests be relegated to second place.

I guess Murray *grew up* with the idea that he was a

swimmer and didn't question it. At all times he was interested and keen to improve while appreciation and the confidence gained by success did much to benefit his naturally shy make-up. There was less and less time for sharing family fun and pleasures, as swimming became the dominant factor in his days, so that the off-season and holidays were doubly enjoyed. For weeks at a time we accustomed ourselves to a breakfast "good morning" and a chat over dinner. Having the beach at our doorstep was a tremendous advantage, one of which Murray and his friends made full use during every spare hour.

Training is the secret of success, but, to a child, training comes a bit hard. Half a mile can seem a long, lonely way to a seven-year-old. It means patience, determination, and the controlling of desires, so during the early stages of practice sessions, I tried to make a point of swimming along, too, for companionship. However, in no time at all, I was left way behind, and, as Murray gradually realized that it was this training that won races, there was no more need for me to be there.

He was fast learning that results can be measured by effort, and finding that never ending strength within himself.

## CHAPTER 6

## *SPORT, THE TEACHER*

Murray's first big test came when he was barely ten years old. All through Australia there is a tremendous emphasis upon sport, and, in Sydney particularly, the swimming championships are looked upon as really important events, covered by press, radio, and television. As the Aussie is well known for his love of a gamble, the big races naturally become the subject of some quite heavy betting. There is always a packed and enthusiastic crowd waiting for the starter's gun.

No matter how we try to toughen our youngsters against such an ordeal, the nervous strain of a first big contest is a formidable one for them to meet. I shall never forget the picture of Murray on the occasion when he faced his first big challenge as, white, trembling, and nearly sick, he anxiously watched for Sam and the strength that came with him.

Knowing his shy and sensitive nature so well, I remember a sense of guilt at having helped bring about what seemed to be almost torture—for have no doubt, it *can* be sheer torture for a while. But with the steadfast assurance of his coach, some of the load was soon lifted.

"Hello boy, come and let's see you in the water! There's no need to worry."

Murray swam a great race, coming a very close second to the reigning champion. What is more, he was over his first big hurdle and went home a truly happy and much stronger boy. In the same event the following year he became the Under-12 champion of New South Wales.

It's a great thing to overcome nerves and acquire courage and control at an early age. Though nervous tension must always remain a part of every contest, you will find that your young athlete soon learns to "take it" and will begin to enjoy the challenge of an important race.

From that time on, Murray faced the championships as an inevitable part of growing up, while trophies and medals began to replace the toys and mechanical models that stood around the shelves of his room. Experts predicted that he could become a great swimmer. As early as 1950 a Sydney columnist, not normally a sports writer, had spotted Murray and was describing him in a Sydney newspaper as "a tow-headed nipper who's just turned 11, stands about as high as our bank balance—quite a little feller. He swims a slow half-mile at Redleaf every morning, a fast half-mile at Bondi every afternoon—and he's been swimming since he was one." Even then, this reporter went as far as advising his readers to back Murray for a title at the 1956 Olympics. Had any taken him seriously, it might well have paid their Olympic expenses!

News reporters made much of Murray's natural diet and seemed fascinated by one item in particular, a sweet, fruity jelly dessert made from the mineral-rich Irish moss (seaweed). In fact, such headings as "The Seaweed Boy" or "Seaweed Streak" began appearing on top of stories about Murray. Truly, seaweed had played quite a part in many ways. Its fresh, tangy smell had floated around him during his first splashing swimming efforts, and when he was playing at the water's edge, it had decorated many a sand castle and make-believe garden. Now it became one of the foods which helped to build health and strength.

Most articles also made some reference to the "fluidity of

his classic style." Perhaps an accomplished swimmer moves most gracefully when he is young, for as muscles develop and greater strength is used, his appearance in the water becomes more one of rhythmic power.

Many people, and I was always one, derive much pleasure from watching good swimming—not only for the excitement of the race but for the rhythmic beauty of movement. I suppose trained co-ordination of the body has the same quality whatever medium it speaks through, for there is always joy in the measured flow of perfected rhythm. We see something of the spirit of man in his striving to overcome limitation and reach out for the best within himself.

The Greeks revered and honored great athletic achievement equally with that in the art or scholastic fields, respecting the mastering of weakness to gain perfection as the true goal and the sphere of accomplishment of secondary importance. What matter if it be through music, science, art, or sport? There is greater satisfaction in watching a classic tennis player than in seeing the clumsy movements of a poor dancer. Or in listening to the mastered tones of a simple native instrument than hearing the discord of an orchestra badly trained.

If we heard of an earthly Shangri-la, it would matter little how we journeyed there. Whether by plane, ship, or traveling on foot, the joy of reaching our goal would be the same. There is a meaning behind sport that is perhaps little realized, though at least one ancient cult of spiritual philosophy has used such mediums as fencing, archery, and other physical arts in order to help man find and master himself. It is in the discipline itself that something deeper can be found and in the patient repetition, day after day, year after year. The rhythmic breathing necessary in conditioning, as well as during performance, steadies and feeds and opens the mind in a way Eastern culture has recognized for centuries.

Then, too, the complete aloneness during the miles of training for building stamina must be conducive to inner thinking, and to serious minds, anyway, it tends to take them beyond the trivia of the day as well as to the quiet places within. Such moments can bring a clearer conception of the true order and values behind our lives—a knowledge to be well used by those whose minds are so tuned.

Having spent many years in close contact with great champions, these are thoughts that I felt from them, but I would not be attempting to give them expression had I not met a certain young writer. He was an exceptionally handsome Hollywood type, and a man of unusual perception. When he seemed eager to talk of his athletic experiences I found myself explaining these theories. Surprisingly, he accepted them with complete understanding and assured me that they were perfectly true. But few, he observed, ever followed through after the disciplined life had been abandoned. He then handed me a little book, *Zen in the Art of Archery*, written by an American professor, Eugen Herrigel, who had studied that art under a great mystical teacher. To anyone interested in probing the subject, his experiences are most enlightening.

There is nothing like achievement to bring a glow of satisfaction and content. Feeling unfulfilled, knowing we are capable of so much more than has been expressed or recognized is surely at the back of most unhappiness. And it matters so little how simple the means we use. Preparing a good meal, putting beauty into a garden, or designing attractive furniture—if the result brings pleasure, a need has been supplied. There is, for every one of us, the perfect expression; a place that only we can fill. If we follow our leads, we shall find that place. The thing man seeks is seeking him. Whatever quality or talent we have, there is a need for it—a destiny to fill, but never one to be forced by the convictions of a stronger will.

Had Alexander Graham Bell not visualized and persisted in his seeking he would never have invented the telephone, while Robert Fulton built the picture of a steamboat in the vapor of a boiling kettle.

A woman often seeks perfect self-expression in becoming a wife, mother, and housekeeper, and there is nothing more dynamic in its power for good than in filling such roles perfectly. Such thoughts are wonderfully epitomized in a version I used to tell Murray of Anatole France's famous story:

## The Little Juggler

One Christmastime a certain poor and wandering juggler arrived at the gates of a secluded monastery. He was cold and hungry, and the weather being raw, the kindly monks invited him to stay with them during the holy season.

The beauty of the religious services and the quietude, whispering through the cloisters, stirred something deep within him—something which he longed to express. It was the custom of the monks to work on some individual project and to donate their handiwork in the chapel on Christmas Day, a gift expressing their love of God and which might hopefully earn the praise of their beloved Prior.

Our little juggler watched Brother Thomas patiently embroidering an altar cloth in gold, while Brother Benedict, a natural musician, spent hours composing a hymn on the chapel organ. Brother Francis, the gardening expert had been secretly growing hothouse roses, and old Brother Angelo was writing a poem to the Christ Child. Each and every friar was absorbed in some creation and rendering it as perfectly as his ability could make it. The juggler became troubled as the day of Christmas offerings drew near. He felt so stupid and hopelessly inadequate among minds and hands so expertly proficient. What could *he* do that would express his gratitude and show, as the Prior had told him, that something of God was within each one?

The bells rang out on Christmas morning, and the brothers took their places in the chapel pews. As, one by one, each brother held out his gift for a blessing, the juggler knew that he too *must* give something. But what could it be? There was but one thing which he had to offer—his art as a juggler. When it came to his turn to go up to the altar he intuitively took out his bright juggling balls and started to perform with dexterity and skill. The brothers were shocked and whispered angrily that such desecration should be allowed to take place. But the juggler was now lost in absorbed concentration. His performance had never reached such perfected control, and his mastery over the swiftly rotating colored balls held a meaning he had not been aware of before. He worked with a joy beyond fatigue. Seeing the anger on the faces of the brothers, the Prior became stern and lifted a hand to order their stillness, until the juggler, ending his act, knelt before the altar with his head reverently bowed. Graciously thanking each for a most beautiful donation, the holy father continued by expressing his grief. "The truth which I have endeavored to impart seems to have been far from understood this morning," he said. "This simple visitor has given us something to be deeply remembered. His abandonment of selfish pride . . . his humble gratitude for a gift most patiently trained to perfection more truly expresses a love of God than any other offering. We are blessed that he was sent to be with us this Christmastime."


## Homeward bound

We had talked so much of England that Murray's imagination must have been alive with pictures of his homeland. Now at last, Ian planned to go to Britain on a business trip which brought the wonderful opportunity for our son to see it again and judge for himself.

Murray, being thirteen years of age at the time, was at a vital stage in his studies, and we realized the harmful effect it might have if he fell too far behind his contemporaries. However, the problem was successfully solved, with the co-operation and help of his headmaster and arrangements were made for him to keep abreast of the full curriculum during the prolonged trip abroad. While at sea, he had regular periods of lessons and homework, and we planned to recruit the aid of suitable teachers wherever it was possible, not overlooking the fact that travel in itself was also a valuable and enriching experience.

As we finally drew into the somber activity of London's Waterloo Station, Murray was looking eagerly out of the boat-train window and attempting to recognize his close, but unremembered, relatives. Familiar scenes reappeared, and I pictured again the bundle of white woolens that was once our infant son, being handed to us through a similar window. And now, returning to this selfsame spot, was the grown edition of that coddled little being—a tall, bronzed youngster, a great and lively companion.

"It all looks pretty dull," was Murray's first reaction. "There seems to be so little color anywhere." He was, in fact, feeling the reverse effect of the vivid brightness which had so impressed us when we first arrived in Sydney. Certainly, after being accustomed to the gay dresses and light suits of the semi-tropics, it was strange to see nothing but the subdued colorings of the waiting crowd, while the burden of war had plainly left its mark and stolen much of the old vitality.

However, family reunions and a granny's happy tears brought warmth enough, and after a first self-conscious weighing up, years of separation quickly fell away in the mutual camaraderie and understanding of a family come together again.

One thing which came as quite a shock to Murray was the many various forms of pronunciation he heard around him. He had always taken it for granted that some form of varsity English was spoken throughout England. No doubt the idea grew because we had rather badgered him about the importance of preserving the English language as it was meant to be spoken. He was amazed to find only a small minority used the clipped Oxford accent we had somehow led him to expect.

As though knowing all about our long-anticipated pleasure at being home again, Britain had seemingly made special preparations and planned the brightest, warmest weather they had enjoyed there for years. It turned out to be the well-remembered sunny summer of 1952. Now came the joy of revisiting those places preserved in our thoughts through the years, and discovering whether affectionate memories had led us to over-paint the pictures passed on to Murray. But we soon found out that England still held the same secret of touching the heart, and our happiness was doubled in having a son to share it all with us. We found the hedgerows as flower-tangled as they'd always been, and the same leafy richness bordered country lanes. We relived so much as we strode across the Sussex Downs and caught again the whimsical mood of little woods.

For me there was a dreamlike quality about this holiday, for everything I most loved had come together. No human could expect to hold such joy for long. Life is ever made up of light and shadow, joy and sadness, day and night. This was a period of the brightest day.

To a youngster brought up in a country too new for monuments of any great age, the ancient remains of past history had especial fascination. One of these old haunts we visited held something of personal significance to Murray, for in the lovely precincts of Beauly Abbey, the name of one of his ancestors, Baron de Ros, was recorded as a witness to the abbey's charter in the year 1200. More than three hundred years later its beauty had been ravaged by the soldiers of Thomas Cromwell acting on the orders of Henry VIII. Looking at the wild flowers growing around the onetime altar steps and the cloister pillars still standing as in reverent thought, it was easy to believe the old guide's story that chanting voices were sometimes heard echoing from these holy remains.

Such living contacts with the past brought a natural interest in his own beginnings, and the ancient crest which Murray wears is more than a mere graduation gift. It is a meaningful symbol with its centuries-old motto inscribed in the ring, "Constant and True."

We revisited, too, a scene that I had looked at daily from the window of my childhood home. This was the deer park surrounding the ruins of a onetime princely manor, the home of Lord and Lady Grey. I was able to point out paths trodden down through bracken along which I had so often walked and remembered sadly a little girl who had been there before me—no other than the Lady Jane Grey, the tragic political victim who, at the age of sixteen, had been made Queen of England for just nine days and then cruelly beheaded. We went into the family chapel where she must often have devoutly prayed and stood at the windows of the main hall, looking out at the strangely mutilated appearance of the oaks growing in the park. Lord Grey, as a grim reminder of this brutal crime, had had every tree beheaded, too, on the day his little daughter had died.

As we walked on through this vast estate we came across a large, flat rock perched on the bank of a stream. I told Murray about the day I had climbed onto its table-smooth surface and there fallen asleep. And of how I awoke to see a sunset-flushed sky and believed that I must have still been dreaming, for all around me deer were standing and rabbits hopping. No doubt they had come for their supper-time drink and I occupied their favorite evening meeting place, but they brought the spell of wonderland with them.

Murray asked more of the early days of the little Jane Grey, and I showed him fields of meadowsweet and butter-cups where she might well have walked to meet one of her teachers who lived near by: Hugh Latimer, who was later martyred for his beliefs. It was he, we are told, who in-structed the child in such subjects as Latin and encouraged her philosophical turn of mind. And so we spent the days, journeying through the pictures of the past and the beauties of the present.

But a growing apprehension took some of the gilt from the brightness of Murray's holiday. He knew, of course, that we had serious thoughts of settling there again, and we were aware of how disturbed he felt about such an idea. After any spontaneous remark of interest or admiration, he always concluded with the reminder: "But it will be good to be home in Sydney again, won't it?"

As a matter of fact, we had always planned on return-ing to England some day and had taken it for granted that our son would finish his education there. With this in mind, we had arranged to visit several of the Great Public Schools. In their ancient heritage and stately beauty, these academies had remained quite unchanged, but, we found, we had not. Our reactions came as a surprise, even to ourselves. After knowing twelve years of the wide-open spaces, in the way of both living and thinking, the con-straint of rather hidebound conventions would not be easy to take. In Murray's case it could even have undone a great deal of good.

It was surprising, too, how often the young pupils there, living in apparent luxury and with the background of a socially accepted school, would envy Murray his life in Australia.

"Half your luck being able to go back there!" was the repeated remark when the youngsters were together.

As our son was at an impressionable age and had never been over-confident, such a change, we reasoned, might well deter rather than advance his future potential. Besides, he had striven so very hard to attain his early goals, and to become an Australian champion. All this he might have lost. We decided we dare not take the risk.

While Ian completed the business part of the trip we made our base at Brighton, the once notorious playground of George IV. Here was the perfect center for all our needs, situated one hour away from London and commercial contacts, with the sea and modern swimming pools close by, while throughout Sussex County there was everything rural and historical to please any taste, from thatched cottages and Elizabethan manor houses to ancient battlegrounds and Roman remains.

Brighton College being almost next door, it was not hard to find the best of tuition to keep Murray up to date with his studies. Here, too, at the well-known swimming club, "The Shiverers," he was able to continue his swimming and spend leisure hours with boys of similar interests. The members trained under the expert supervision of Carl Wootton, a knowledgeable and much traveled businessman who was also a dedicated believer in the unique all-round benefits of swimming as a sport. His regular articles on the subject are internationally known and equally his many years of devoted work in this field.

He kindly kept an eye on Murray during his period there, and, after returning to our home down under, we read of his thoughts in the English *Swimming Times*.

"In the early summer of 1952 a tall, blond boy, physically well developed and looking more than his bare 13 years, came to me

at the King Alfred, Hove, and joined the Shiverers. His name
was Murray Rose. He was an English boy who had gone to
Australia at an early age and was then on a visit home with his
parents. . . . As soon as I had seen him in the water a few times
I formed the opinion that he was the finest potential swimmer I
had ever seen anywhere, at home or abroad. His natural aptitude
was near perfection and was only equalled by his mental attitude.
His modest bearing and his willing and untiring response to
every call made on him made him the coaches' ideal. . . . I did
not attempt to interfere with the technique of his stroke but just
had him swimming long easy distances with our boys so that he
would be in good condition on his return to Australia. . . . The
Australian press is now hailing Murray as 'the greatest swimming
prospect Australia has had.' My own opinion, based not on
performances but on my assessment of his potentialities and
character, is that in due course, Murray Rose will reach world-
record form."

Australia and swimming called us back, and the day
came sadly for Ian and me when we had to part once
again from the land we most loved and the warmth of being
close to our families. The roses of farewell which we found
in our cabin brought a heartache that has never quite
healed. On one side of the ocean was tender intimacy of
things we knew and understood, while on the other was
vigorous, healthy living and the promise of success. But
after this second upheaval it seemed that our roots would
not take a firm hold again.

## CHAPTER 7

## NATURE, THE MASTER COACH

I think we always knew that fate had it planned for us to make our home in America one day. We had, in fact, made every attempt to reach that country when we first left England during World War II, but currency and immigration regulations made it an impossibility then. We were further delayed by falling under the spell of Australia's un-fenced-in mental attitude: its carefree outdoor living, idyllic weather, and the endless stretches of glorious surfing beaches.

But now our thoughts were taking a definite shape and setting the scene for a future in the United States. For a while yet, our young champion would need our full recourses of time, energy, and money, and there could have been no happy change until our shared goal had been reached. In a way, it could be said that our journey to the States took seventeen years to complete, a journey packed full of unexpected twists and rich discoveries.

The season of championship meets was approaching at the time of our return to Sydney, which meant Murray must get straight into a severe conditioning and training program and the household back into a strict routine. Unlike America, there is only one championship swimming season down under, and that a long and arduous one. Here in the States there are the summer meets, held in outdoor long-course (50-meter) pools, which climax in July and

August, and winter competition as well, which takes place in indoor short-course (generally 25-meter) pools. Racing in these short-course pools often "throws" an overseas athlete at first, as his experience has almost always been gained entirely in the longer pools, which are mandatory in all serious international competition and the only pools in which world records are now recognized.

Perhaps it was just as well that we came back to Australia at the hardest period of the year—for me at any rate—because this meant fewer idle moments which might have been spent remembering. During this time, when the accent must be on swimming and the building of physical stamina, it is not always easy to maintain the balance between study, athletics, and relaxation which we knew to be desirable. This distribution of energies can become a most complex problem in the background of any athlete and one many parents find hard to resolve.

We recall several occasions when we have sat with the parents of a competitor at athletic meets or football games and seen them almost hysterical with desire for their youngsters to do well. Yet a few weeks later we have met those same parents and heard them anxiously bemoan the fact that their boy's grades were not as high as they wished. What *do* wise parents truly wish for their children? A balance of both, I imagine, and the attainment of this is greatly influenced by their own understanding and behavior. There is a time and the ability to achieve each worthwhile goal but not necessarily at the same moment. It is a fact that a fit and well-co-ordinated body also aids brain activity and balance of mind.

The Russians have done a great deal of study on the relationship between brain and muscles and affirm that physical exercise recharges the brain. But the availability of time must obviously dictate the priority of the moment. In Murray's case, we tried to take the long-term point of view and not expect the top in every activity simultaneously. For instance, during the season of intensive swimming training we did not look for high scholastic achievement. Perhaps because he knew this and did not feel that pressure was being applied—which so often results in tense, frustrated reactions—he always managed to keep above average in his grades.

If any subject seemed to be falling off, then we arranged for extra coaching during the off-season or vacation periods. By placing an equal importance on both study and sport and by appreciating and sharing in their efforts to succeed, youngsters, in time, will inevitably want to acquire knowledge for themselves. But we must try to refrain from "getting on their backs" in either sphere of activity. If the will to reach the top is within their make-up, it will eventually be expressed.

Parents become emotionally, as well as practically involved, in the pre-championship preparations, and I have never yet known a champion who doesn't become taut and intensely apprehensive as the challenge draws near. All we parents can do is to quietly absorb some of that tension with understanding. Though they might not know it at the time, and our efforts may fall very short of their need, every thought and every service is directed to give extra backing of help, strength, and complete belief in them.

In a way we ourselves had added to the responsibility by adopting a somewhat unorthodox diet. In fact, a question repeatedly demanding an answer, not only for the many who posed it but for ourselves as well, has been: "How does Murray get his food when he has to swim away from home?" How indeed?

Every far distant meet was a real challenge to ingenuity and planning. We learned mostly through mistakes and unhappy experience, but it was never easy. As it happened, the very year we returned from England brought the first of such challenges. That year, the Australian championships were of especial importance because successful contenders would be chosen to compete in the British Commonwealth Games to be held later in Vancouver. When it was announced that this meet would take place in Melbourne, some six hundred miles from our home, we decided to do the best we could—but that best was not nearly good enough.

Queen Elizabeth and Prince Philip were visiting Melbourne at the same time, bringing the usual big influx of visitors, so we were lucky to obtain, after much difficulty, accommodation in a hotel about four miles from the pool and the team's headquarters. There, with the help of a smuggled-in hot plate (any cooking by guests being prohibited in this luxury establishment) we struggled to prepare at least some of the foods Murray needed. Murray himself, still too young to hold a driving license, had to make his way through the crowds that waited at every vantage point, hoping for a glimpse of the royal entourage.

During the first races of the series, while still able to draw upon energies previously built up, Murray held his own. But as the days of the championships wore on, his strength grew less and his times slowed down. The experience, however, was by no means without its benefits, for it made us determined that on similar occasions in the future our plans would have to be far more constructive— we hoped! At least we resolved that when *important* swimming events were scheduled away from home, it was imperative for me to set up a suitable base from which our established regime could be continued, and I became, for a time, something of a mobile parent.

During the annual championships next year we tried hard to improve on any lack of organization. This time, the titles were fought out in Adelaide, the capital of Southern Australia, a city where natural health principles were then almost unheard of.

Knowing it to be a place which was geographically isolated, we took along most of the hard-to-get food items, though not, unfortunately, a juicing machine. When we arrived, the summertime heat was at a sweltering peak. I can still feel the cling of damp clothes and the foot-burning sidewalks as I spent the best part of the first few days in search of freshly squeezed carrot juice—an item which had become such an everyday part of our diet that I thought of it in almost prosaic terms.

Carrot juice or elephant milk—it was all the same; there was mighty little difference to the people of Adelaide. Wherever I went, I kept up a single-minded inquiry—in trams, at the post office, in shops, just about everywhere. Finally, when buying (of all commonplace things) a reel of cotton to sew on a championship badge, I struck a promising trail.

The salesgirl had read about Murray and knew about his special diet, and, what was more to the point, her boss actually had a friend who had been cured of gastric ulcers by drinking large quantities of raw vegetable juice. We were on to it at last. She introduced me to her manager who made many phone calls on my behalf. The generosity of these people who gave their time during the rush hour in a busy store was the sort of incident which keeps our picture of humanity in true focus.

Eventually I did track down a juicing machine—one which had changed hands many times and which had, I felt sure, the dubious distinction of being the only electric juice extractor in Adelaide. I discovered it in a cafe attached to the local YWCA, and early every morning I took the tram across the city to pick up the freshly squeezed juice. Under the circumstances, I decided to forget all about

searching for our usual supply of goat's milk and similar
esoteric items!

Those prehistoric trams of Adelaide—I can hear them still
as they rattled and grated up the steep hill outside the
building which was our temporary home, while all through
the night giant interstate trucks seemed headed straight
for my window. Counting sheep and using wax ear stops
proved of little help, but I suppose it was all a part of
the price of being a "member" of a team at an age when
one should have been content to stay quietly at home!
But somehow it all worked out, and wonderfully well,
for when we boarded the plane that would take us back
home—and to Ian—Murray had become the first Junior
swimmer to become freestyle champion of Australia over
five different distances.

In this day and age, and especially in America, it would
all have been so much easier. But when we began our new
way of life, almost a quarter of a century ago, Australia
was still in the dark ages where health foods were concerned, and meat was the major part of every meal for
most people, including even steak for breakfast. The produce we sought was impossible to come by at any of the
regular food shops or markets. Items such as millet and
sunflower seeds were literally "for the birds," and if we
inquired for such things as sesame or tahini we were almost regarded as beings from outer space. The difficulties
seemed unsurmountable. Had it not been for our friends
who "pioneered" along with us, and our regained vitality
and health, we might have been discouraged in our efforts.

As it was, we persisted in our questioning and searched
through immigrant areas, unknown to us before, in tracking
down the hideout of many of our needs. Climbing a narrow staircase we found an attic store run by Greeks which
turned out to be a rendezvous for hundreds of new arrivals

Murray enjoyed football, riding, and other sports before giving everything to swimming.

Murray was barely ten years old at the time of his first big championship swim. *(Photo by Associated Newspapers Ltd., Sydney)*

More healthful relaxation, in the Blue Mountains.

Right from the start the fluidity of his classic style was the subject of constant comment. (*Sydney* Morning Herald *photo*)

A rare break between training, study, and championship swimming—enjoying the peace of an "undiscovered" Pacific island, the home of an artist friend.

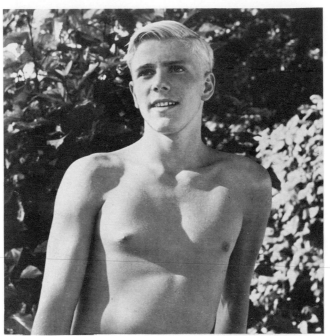

As the Greeks discovered long ago, sun, water, and air are beneficial gods indeed. *(Photo by Doug Balmer)*

Being captain of the school swimming team meant happy days and many warm memories. *(Photo by Melba Studios, Sydney)*

First representing the state of New South Wales in a national championship.

It was impossible to think of Murray without Sam Herford, or Sam without Murray. *(Photo by Associated Newspapers Ltd., Sydney)*

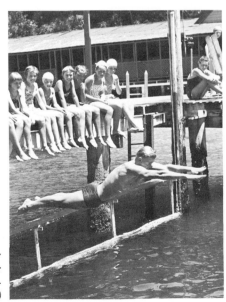

At Sam Herford's baths, Murray worked alongside yet a further group of friends. *(Photo by Associated Newspapers Ltd., Sydney)*

Murray finally chose the University of Southern California as his alma mater. (*Photo by Phil Bath for* Sports Illustrated)

Murray put in extra study to make up for the tremendous digressions into the world of sport. *(Photo by permission of Australian News and Information Bureau)*

When I unpacked the T-shirts Murray wore during workouts, I could wring out the perspiration. *(Sydney Morning Herald photo)*

to the country—and where tahini and sesame were everyday purchases. From oriental shopkeepers we obtained millet, brown, unpolished rice, and edible seaweeds, while the Italian stores supplied us with unsaturated oils, goat's milk, and unpasteurized cheese.

Finding the foods was by no means the end. Since natural produce was not always prepared for human consumption it was necessary to grind the grains, and dehull the millet and sunflower seeds. And the vegetable juice was usually squeezed in a hand machine. I remember how we often talked of our experiments, hoping that in some way they might throw a little light on how to eliminate much disease and build up physical resources. If we can judge from the many encouraging letters and from the reports of health stores, then some of these hopes have indeed materialized. We hear that Murray's successes in the Olympic Games, and the resultant publicity for his way of life, has had a real impact on the health food business. A living example can be immediately understood.

With a growing interest in matters of health and food it became progressively easier to obtain the goods for which we once spent hours and energy searching. Even so, during the 1960 Olympics in Rome, the clock was turned right back and we found ourselves struggling again in a background similar to those old conditions. Though this experience came some years after our present story, I am recounting it here merely to show how our pattern of nonconformity continued to bring problems along with its undeniable joys.

By the time of this XVII Olympiad we were pretty much in the spotlight as far as Murray's unorthodox way of life was concerned. We felt the heavy responsibility of proving the validity of these ideologies, for we never lacked critics who were ready to judge if the slightest cause arose.

We were somewhat prepared for the difficulties ahead

but not for the epic obstacle race it turned out to be. Not being on particularly intimate terms with the Eternal City and realizing that the language barrier would be an extra hazard, we had shipped a quantity of foods from America. Ian, flying in from New York to join us after many months of separation, came with suitcases and pockets bulging with still more important food items. At the same time, I was arriving in Rome after the long training period in Australia and adding further to the food store in our antiquated Roman apartment, even bringing loaves of our own special bread which were still fresh enough to eat eighteen days later.

Even with all these preparations, there were many things for which we had to depend on local supplies. It took us quite a number of days, for instance, to ferret out an elusive little health store (one of the very few) in the maze of narrow streets which adjoin the "Three Coins" fountain.

Our efforts at positive thinking were to be tested a thousand ways, too, by such things as the fortuitous plumbing which often gave up entirely by midday, by a water supply which had to be supplemented by jugs and buckets filled from a tap on the roof of the apartment building, and by the appalling noise which drifted through our windows, always open because of the heat of Rome in August. Immediately below us there was an auto-repair shop which obviously did not lack work and, adjacent to it, a barracks where army trucks trundled in and out, discharging and picking up members of the Italian soldiery. Barely a hundred meters from our windows was the only open-air movie theater in the neighborhood, which entertained its patrons until midnight. Worst of all, was the tall sentinel that overlooked us—the campanella of the local church that was to chastise both the wicked and the good with an iron tongue, beginning at 5:45 A.M. every day.

Our concern for Murray was not improved by the knowledge that the Australian team, on its way to Rome, had been grounded in Bahrein through engine trouble and spent many hours stewing in the heat of the Persian Gulf. This was the last straw and a situation which could have seriously affected the razor-sharp form of mettlesome athletes. When they finally did land, sleep and a peaceful background were vital to quick recovery. We could offer little of either.

There were many weary and anxious hours during the Rome games which are best not recorded. But Murray's defense of his 400-meter title most definitely was recorded—and around the world—for it made him the first swimmer in the history of the Games to have won a long-distance event in two successive Olympics. However, as previously explained, this was four years and many contests later than the events recorded here.

When we finally settled in the United States, many of our headaches were over, at least as far as the dietary worries were concerned. After visiting several of the great universities Murray chose the University of Southern California in Los Angeles, not only because of its high academic standards or the perfect all-year climate but also because of the broad-minded understanding of his needs. He was, in fact, supplied with practically the same diet which he was accustomed to having, although obtaining enough strength-giving foods when competing in distant swim meets has continued to be a constant tax on Murray's energies and ingenuity.

Of course we ran up against the same opposition to any unorthodox and different way of thinking, the same domination by organized controlling bodies whose main mission, it seemed to us, was that of blocking enlightenment to the benefit of following nature's own principles. There was, however, an increasing interest in natural health foods, especially in California, and a growing disquiet that modern scientific methods which included "protective" shots, repressive drugs, and chemicalized, processed products were not by any means the answer to preserving health or eliminating disease and suffering. Many were beginning to look for a better way—and to examine what natural principles had to offer.

We cannot fail to see the inspired genius behind Science which has done so much to enrich our lives, nor be other than deeply grateful for the miracles it has worked in changing matter into forms of tremendous advantage to us. It has turned matter into machines that replace the labor of man; brought means of reaching any place on earth—and out of it; and the ability to speak instantaneously to another, wherever he may be. But when it comes to trying to control the workings of the body by the use of chemicals, then it has not been wholly successful. Medicine and drugs cannot bring about new and complete health, because they represent an attempt to transform matter by matter. And we are far more than just matter. We cannot be kept fit and well adjusted merely by means of scientific formulas. Our life-force depends on principles more perfect than these. In this sort of training, nature is undoubtedly the master coach.

There is one healing magic that has never been surpassed, and that is the healing, guiding power of love. Seeming miracles have been worked by love where other methods have failed, for it recruits the aid of the Supreme Physician. In other than physical suffering, too, there is no wiser therapy. When a friend is discouraged, or a little one is afraid, love inspires the words to bring a change of heart.

Praise is a remedy we might also use more often. Every parent has experienced its transforming effect. What we don't always realize is that we can also administer praise to ourselves. There are times when criticism or condemnation have left us with a sense of failure, and we become depressed about our own limitations. It is then that we can praise that which *we* know ourselves to be, the intelligence which is as much a part of us as of anyone else. This is one of the keys that Jesus left with us when He said: "I speak not for myself, but the Father abiding in me doeth His Works." This repeated thought quickly brings self-belief and a stream of helpful ideas. But whether we give it to ourselves, or to one who looks to us for help, we shall find hope and success growing out of praise.

Far from bringing us a sense of well-being, present-day conditions tend to weaken our faith. Fear of disease, especially, is set before us across the pages of almost each newspaper and magazine we happen to pick up; it is radioed into our consciousness with every news bulletin, and it creeps into the intervals between TV programs. Of all the "killers" we are constantly warned as likely to visit our homes, the one against which we should be most on guard is the catching of fear itself. Fear can fatally draw us to the very thing we fear.

We must take dominion over destructive forces—claim peace and freedom from constant anxiety. Each individual is ultimately responsible for his own success, his own undisturbed peace of mind, his own bodily health—and for his part in bringing the overtones of well-being into his home and the world as a whole.

When I think of the enormous cost of penetrating outer space—not only in money, but in the expenditure of energy, creative talent and even human life, I can't help seeing the sizable unfinished job of straightening out man's problems here. If, by penetrating a tiny part of the infinite mysteries beyond, man can also penetrate the infinities within himself, then he would leave a rich heritage indeed for his children and the children after that.

CHAPTER 8

## BECOMING A STAR

Young hopefuls had been training with a purpose for the summer championships of 1955. Australian sportsmen everywhere were stimulated by the knowledge that theirs was to be the host country for the coming Olympic Games, well over a year away. This was the first time they had gained such an honor; indeed it was the first time the Games had been held in the Southern Hemisphere. Sir Frank Beaurepaire, the man largely responsible for this achievement, had been one of the leading swimmers for Australia at the Olympics in 1908 and up to 1920. So the swimmers, especially, had a torch to carry.

This meet lived up to its promise of being one of excitement. Many thrilling and unexpected results were recorded, and great champions were toppled. Murray was one who happened to do some of the toppling. Though still a Junior, he swam in the Senior Events and amazed the crowd by making his first Australian record in the 440-yard race.

Spurred and encouraged, he also succeeded in capturing the 880-yard Australian race, becoming a star overnight. "Sydney's new swim idol," ran the headline of a newspaper at the time, and the secretary of the State Swimming Association reported that Murray's performance was "better than that of any of the place-getters at the last Olympic Games."

Murray soon had invitations to swim in other states of

Australia and almost immediately found himself in Queensland for the Swimming Carnival at Brisbane. The sporting fans of the *Courier Mail* in that city read in its February 2 issue: "Australia's new sensational swim find was in town. He arrived in Brisbane yesterday, with coach Sam Herford, to compete in the Queensland swim titles. Within half an hour he was working at the Valley pool. Rose, although a youngster, looks the type Hollywood producers would like to get. He is a powerfully built 6 ft. blond. His physique is perfect. Rose has a chest measurement of 42 inches. He weighs 164 pounds.

"The way he has been swimming this season, Rose looks a big chance for the 1956 Melbourne Olympic Games. Coach Herford told me that Rose could have reached the top before this season, but he has held him back. Said Herford 'For 11 years now I have been looking after Murray and I know his potential. That is the reason why I have kept him until this season—and this is only the start of his career.'

"Rose had about half as much training as other topflight swimmers for his records this season. He is keen on study and does not let schooling miss out because of his sporting activities. Rose is a sensation now because he has great natural stamina, wonderful physique, and because of the fact that he wants to reach the top.

"Another thing in his favor is that Herford has not bustled him. He has been allowed to develop gradually."

"Heavy is the head . . ."

Success and honor can be quite a load to carry. The responsibility of not just racing but being expected to *win* every time, and make new records too, is a strain on any youngster. But that is the price of being a reigning champion. (Murray has now had fourteen years of finding this out.)

He was very young then and seriously conscientious and fully appreciative of the many who believed in him and backed him all the way. He spared nothing of himself so as not to let them down. There was one important freestyle event well worth recording—for in it was a vital part of the molding process, a process whereby we often gain when we are apparently the loser. Ill with influenza at the time, he knew how much this race meant to his opponents and keenly wished to compete. Against all advice, he got up out of bed with a reeling head and aching limbs and insisted on doing the best he could.

The press on such occasions can be devastating, as all true sportsmen know. "Rose yesterday gave a puzzling display to finish a distant third in the 1650 yards . . . He swam erratically throughout and covered much more distance than any of his rivals," said the main Sydney newspaper.

The merits of a true champion can be known only to those closest to him. Such reports served merely to strengthen his resolution, and two days later, still far from well, he swam what many officials describe as "the most courageous race of his career" in the 880-yard championship to beat his former victors. Only recently an Australian swimming expert who was visiting the United States recalled this race, reiterating that to him and many others, this was the greatest swim he had ever witnessed.

A few weeks later Murray was to break the world record for the 1650 yards too.

Any youngster with a halo of world renown naturally becomes a hero among his school fellows. But of greater importance is a well-earned respect for weathering the tough grounding that put him where he is. Because of this, it comes easier for an athlete to assume a position of responsibility with confidence and understanding, whether his role lies in the sporting, civic, or academic field.

During his life at Cranbrook, a famous private school overlooking the beauty of Sydney harbor, Murray learned much in all three spheres. As a member of the school committee he had practice in thinking and planning for a community. Being a school prefect gave him experience in a more executive capacity while as a sports captain, he learned something of leadership and passing on encouragement to others.

Being Captain of Swimming for Cranbrook School and later for the University of Southern California probably gave Murray some of the happiest days and warmest memories of his life. We, too, were privileged to be a part of some of these rich experiences. There was one day in particular when we more subdued adult onlookers had been deeply stirred by the unquenchable enthusiasm of youth.

It all began on a ferryboat especially chartered to take the boys over the harbor to the Olympic Pool where the biggest Swimming Carnival of the school season was taking place. This was a pretty important day for Murray, not only as captain of the team, but because it would be the last time he would swim for his school. Although the Olympic Games were but a few months away, his main concern and interest had been the training of the school swimmers for this event. Every morning before breakfast the youngsters had been put through their paces. In the evenings Murray continued his own conditioning program. The boys had tried their hardest during the short time they'd had to prepare, and, as soon as they had come aboard the boat, one could feel the excitement of keen anticipation. An old piano had been left from some previous outing, and a young pianist quickly supplied a suitable outlet for the gathering tensions. The boys began singing tune after tune until they came to the stirring rhythm of the "Eton Boating Song."

As we swayed with the rhythm of the swelling waves and the moving chorus of young voices, we parents, too, were caught up in the fervors of the song, and not one of us there could have given words to the overwhelming feeling it brought.

It was our own youth echoing back. It was all the hope we knew for these boys of ours. In it was not only the pledge of strength for the coming schoolboy contests but the expression of ideals and buoyant faith that every heart starts out with. And as the ferryboat drew into the quay beside the swimming stadium, an eager mood of expectation had been set.

Seven schools were gathered there, each with a large following of enthusiastic supporters. Two of those schools were outstanding in swimming, with several potential Olympic champions as members of their team.

As the band played and cheerleaders led each school in its own chanting "war song," the blazing sunshine brought the background scene sharply into focus. Ships starting out across the world would silently glide past, but the spectators were too engrossed to notice them. As the races proceeded Cranbrook managed to hold their own and, point by point, quite unexpectedly kept up with their competitors. Murray and his teammates had carefully planned their strategy so that every split second's worth of advantage could be gained.

Murray never left the sidelines between his own races and was as keenly absorbed as we had ever seen him. With his arm around the shoulders of some tense competitor or whispering encouragement to a very young starter, it seemed he was trying to pass on strength as it so often had been given to him.

Cranbrook were running neck and neck with their formidable rivals, and with only the last few races left to be swum the growing excitement became intense. In the last stroke of the final thrilling struggle they gained the one point needed to win the day, and the tears of sheer joy in the smallest one's eyes are somehow very dear to remember.

Among the many souvenirs carefully preserved as poignant mementos are the thoughts of a previous Cranbrook captain written to Murray on that day:

"As a former Captain of Swimming, it was plain that you had the whole of your team right behind you. To have done this, you must have been perfect in your job as Captain. It was difficult for you, since you were away at an important time, and so the credit to you must be even greater.

"I have heard people say that Murray Rose won the Carnival for Cranbrook, but this is not so. He had a great deal to do with it, but it was the Captain of the Swimming Team who won the Carnival . . . and it is the Captain who deserves the credit. Congratulations, Murray!"

## CHAPTER 9

## DRAWING MUSIC FROM THE MIND

On looking back I realize that perhaps we didn't take formal scholastic education quite as heavily as some parents do. In spite of this, maybe even *because* of it, Murray always worked hard and managed to hold his own. In his case, of course, there were tremendous digressions into the world of sport, and concessions had to be made in order to encompass the hours of training necessary as well as periods away at important swimming championships. Murray put in all the extra study possible and successfully completed the school syllabus.

As things turned out, sport itself proved to be one of the greatest and most helpful teachers of all, not only in producing health and physical strength but in maturing the heart and mind as well as the body. Though some educators are reluctant to recognize the unparalleled benefits that come through the ideals of top-level sport, others are quick to acknowledge its worth in cultivating many valuable qualities necessary in the making of a well-rounded adult.

True over-all education surely means far more than training the brain to become an automatic computer of second-hand facts and figures. It means the wise and benevolent tending of an unfolding life—persuading it to grow to its full potential. It means inducing an awareness of the miracle of the mind by casting light on to its subtle but immense powers.

In much the same way that a flower will not open if exposed to freezing winds, so these intrinsic powers may be paralyzed by wrong and unfavorable conditions.

A wise bringing up will not "untune" the heart but will draw from it the finest and sweetest that is there.

It is not in tradition, or systems of teaching, that wisdom is to be found, though these may be valuable in pointing the way. The ability of the mind to steer its own thinking, and to discern truth in every form and disguise, is the invaluable gift of a man who has learned to "see" for himself. Youthful impressions go very deep, and those first years of guiding by parents and teachers can bring riches or poverty in their true sense.

My own schooldays in England, like those of many others, were hampered by conformities and rigidly fixed rules. It took a pretty determined spirit, as my contemporaries will agree, to shine its way through the thick veils of convention and the narrow, self-determined opinions that prevailed.

Our teachers themselves were dedicated souls, but they belonged to a system which stunted individual growth. These "experienced" adults, chosen as our examples, had to be accepted as knowing the ultimate of right and wrong. Intuitive thoughts, pleading for expression, were all too often rather brutally choked back, or, if we spontaneously showed enthusiasm of an unconventional nature, we were coldly reprimanded and put into "our place"—a place that, forever after, is hard to climb out of.

We all of us view our childhood days with very mixed emotions and most of us carry over a definite sense that a great deal within us was never brought out. The awareness of this hindered growth gives enlightened leads when the job of tending our own little ones is entrusted to us.

Only now, when my life is over the halfway mark am I beginning to comprehend some of the reasons behind many mistakes and disappointments. Wisdom comes to the world from those deeply inspired from within, those enlightened enough to communicate something of the One All-Knowing Mind.

How often we read or hear of a completely "new" slant on some subject and are immediately aware that we've known this to be so all along—though we've never brought it to the surface of our minds before! We come to this earth with natural wisdom; intuitive knowledge already implanted within us. We do not develop new qualities so much as we unfold and extend that which is eternally existent.

In many ways, the present scholastic system with its memory tests and cramming for examinations does little to encourage thoughts of a more profound, enlightened, and meditative nature. So many facts, skills, and technicalities have to be acquired in order to exist in an intensively competitive world, that the way of self-inquiry can be somewhat hampered unless we parents instill the need of deeper wisdom. Not so much by emphasizing the great importance of it as by seeing that the natural channels are kept open.

Children instinctively desire to seek the meaning behind all they see and hear, often to an extent which is beyond our ability to give complete enlightenment. But there are great teachings and philosophies whose ageless wisdom is always available to reach and awaken the mind to do its own thinking—these and the loving contemplation of nature.

There are times when we think we make tremendous discoveries but usually it's just that the pressures have dropped away. There are people, and even places, that seem especially able to do this for us. I recall the impact of just such a place—a certain "undiscovered" island in the Pacific where we just "let go" because there was nothing else that we could do. The unpressured remoteness of this place, the hushed stillness that dominated one's every thought was an experience which is becoming rare indeed to find.

There was no official transport by which to reach this island. It had no modern roads—only soundless, sandy paths. Not one revving motor or blaring car horn ever disturbed its peace. And without the encroaching sounds of any neighbor's TV or radio set, one became aware of the subtler tones coming from the island itself—music to which one might tune at any time, day or night.

An artist friend lived alone on this island for the greater part of his life. It was through him we managed to obtain a bungalow situated on the beach which, unbelievable though it sounds, had running water and modern facilities installed by a previously wealthy owner.

As we walked with our friend through the thick tropical forest, he would point out how the many needs of man were growing there—not only in the way of food and drink, but, when you knew where to look, and how to use them, curative medicines and healing balms which could be obtained from the leaves, and barks, and roots. Even beauty secrets were always on hand.

One day we discovered the remains of a once charming home and many signs of what had been a large and abundant garden. On making inquiries, we learned that many years before a journalist of middle age had been told that he was dying, and with his wife and one old servant had set sail from the mainland of Australia on a last adventure. He had landed on this island and started a new life close to nature, eating the simplest of home-grown foods and had enjoyed life as never before for a further thirty-odd years.

This garden became our local store. We dug taro and yams from the earth, picked mangoes, papayas, bananas, and wild berries, and made a delectable cream from the coconuts which fell from the palms around this, or our own tropic home. Occasionally the artist would take his boat to the mainland and sail back with any extra items we happened to fancy.

A champion can never quite forget the responsibility of keeping himself fit and having some sort of "work out" every day. For exercise we swam in the clear rock pools, and swung on the thick vines that hung from the trees, or climbed around the sea's edge, adding to our collection of rare shells.

It was here that we met a path-maker—in more senses than one. Almost daily we ran into this unforgettable character—a workman whose job was that of making new paths and keeping them safe to walk on. We found it fascinating to watch him making charming rustic furniture from the materials which grew in the forest—cane, wood, and reeds —even using giant beans to decorate his creations. It became very clear, after a few conversations, that he'd also acquired a depth of philosophy one rarely finds in any sphere of life.

His most prized possessions, we soon found out, were his much-worn books by ancient Greek thinkers. These he studied, and thought about constantly, during the many lonely hours of his hermit-like life.

In the cool of the evenings he would often come to help us build a fire outside our home, and add experienced tips on the most appetizing way of cooking our supper over it.

We might express our wonder at the exquisite design of a shell which had just been added to Murray's collection. "Not one," he reminded us, "is ever identical with another. The artistry of the Creator is not repeated in any form of nature. Such perfected genius is beyond man's comprehension. Our greatest minds are still intent on fathoming its secrets. What human scientist, for instance, can explain the mystery of photosynthesis—that process by which plants change sunlight into chlorophyll? Where comes the inspiration for the geometrical poetry of a snowflake? And who tells the swallow that it is time to return home on March 19?"

He had come to see that nature, beneath its confused surface, had a clear and simple pattern of law and order, and he believed, that as man strove to understand the grand design, his own sense of limitation began little by little to fall away from him. He showed us that most of our thinking today in such areas as theology and nuclear physics, in which many believe we are pioneering, had been known centuries ago by mental giants like Plato and Aristotle. Universal truths, it seems, have always been clearly comprehended by certain great sages.

We asked him for his definition of God and what power was ruling over our Universe. He believed that the most logical answer had been supplied by the Greek thinker, Anaximander, whose finding was that all things obeyed a built-in rule and that this divine principle of law and order was embodied in the Boundless which "comprehends" all things and steers the whole. These, and many other thoughts, he passed on for us to ponder over. He more than made up for any lack of social contacts and mental stimulus.

Three or four people was the biggest crowd we saw, except when a pearl diving lugger would drop anchor in order to replenish her water supply. Then the Thursday islanders aboard provided entertainment never bettered for us in the plushest night clubs or from the most expensive theater seats. Their stage was our palm-studded beach, and their decor the moonlit ripples of a tropic surf. Dressed as simply as possible, and with white bandannas to hold back their streaming hair, they would sway and move to the emotionally stirring music of their native songs.

These visitors offered us a sight-seeing tour not included in official guide books. When we boarded their craft very early one morning, we found it scrubbed spotlessly clean for the occasion, and we were deeply touched by the fresh, wild orchids which had been painstakingly entwined around masts and ropes. We cruised around islands which were even more remote, and explored their strange, wild beauty that appeared quite untouched by man.

In our home today, stored alongside the crates of medals and silver cups are boxes of shells which we brought from this Barrier Reef region—exotically rare, and some of them collector's items, we are told. To us they are reminders of a state of serenity which mounting pressures, all too frequently, cause us to forget.

## The Imprint of Parents

I have always believed that there is some very important reason why we are the parents of the particular little beings who come to us. There is nothing haphazard or capricious about the Universal laws. There must be some underlying and age-old pattern why we are the ones chosen to supply the experience and help they most need.

If the depth of sensitivity of a little child is overlooked or not sufficiently comprehended, the spirit can be dangerously crushed. At least this was so when I was young.

I remember a painful example of this at the time I was recovering from a childhood illness. I was given the "great honor" of being allowed to recuperate at the vast home of a most respected and wealthy relative. Here, I found myself cut off from all that was tender, warm and healing. I was constantly rebuked if, unknowingly, I stepped over the invisible line which separates a well-behaved child from an adult. I was repeatedly admonished for my lack of appreciation of my own good fortune, and the great kindness of my elders. But of what value, to a sick and lonely child, are rich furnishings, wide staircases, long, cold corridors, servants, and a remote, socially correct grown-up world? This grand home housed but one toy, a valuable 200-year-old doll, which of course must never be played with; only occasionally looked at in the presence of an adult. Frigid silence met my tearful pleas to go home until, one wonderful day, I saw the familiar kind face of the baker who delivered bread to my parents who lived on the other side of the town. Frightened but desperate, I hid in his horse-drawn cart, later to appear and beg him to take me home. My worthy, well-meaning aunt never really forgave me for the rest of her days.

That bridge of tenderness and the recognition that both child and adult are equally important individuals, supplies the magic key to childhood growth and happiness and establishes a mutual respect and thoughtfulness.

The *motive* behind youngsters' behavior is the all-important factor. Too often they are punished for something which actually stems from an intuitive desire to do right.

There was the time, for instance, when I was fretting about a wild bird which had been captured and placed into a very small cage, and hung outside the door of a relative's house. So obsessed did I become with the conviction that it was my job to free this imprisoned little life that I could neither sleep nor concentrate on studies. Finally, on a day when I knew the family to be out, I crept off from school, made the long journey to their home, and threw open the door of the constricting box which had cramped wings created for flying. So often had I imagined this moment that it had become imperative for my peace of mind. Never will I forget the way that bird almost unbelievingly flew out; nor how, for a moment, it interrupted its flight, perched on a nearby branch, and whistled seemingly in joyous gratitude before soaring off to its rightful freedom.

No matter what reprimand was to follow, something inside felt glad.

Parents leave an imprint upon us for life, and the design of this "rubber stamp" probably makes its mark through the generations to follow.

It was my mother, no doubt, who prepared the ground for my easy acceptance of a natural way of life. She was intrinsically a child of nature and was frequently teased about her "gypsy blood." It was she who scorned medicaments and confinement in bed when we suffered from minor childhood ills but resorted instead to the healing properties of herbs and fresh air, taking us to the top of the highest nearby hill in order to "blow away" a cold, or after miles of walking in heavy English brogues, would join us as we dipped our tired feet into the cool, soothing water of a stream or bubbling spring. During the hot weather she brewed a wonderfully thirst-quenching drink made from fresh dandelions and young nettles and gathered wild rose hips in the fall to be turned into a protective potion which today would be considered the finest source of vitamin C.

My father was an athlete born and showed great potential in many fields but was discouraged from developing so impractical a gift. (He never knew the love and care of his mother.) His own father, coming from the identical mold as the notorious Mr. Barrett of Wimpole Street, sternly repressed every natural desire in each member of his large Victorian family. We were blessed with the most devoted father this side of heaven, a man sensitive and generous to a fault. Tragically, the pressure of this fear-ridden world became too much for his highly-tuned nature, and the added wartime anxieties impelled him to escape altogether. While we ran freely along the stretches of sun-kissed Australian sand, he was to take his precious life—a life deeply needed by us who loved him so much. Had he only realized that clouds *always* move away, and the warmth of happiness ever awaits to take their place, I am sure that he would have stayed around a little longer. But a measure of himself lives on in a champion grandson whose goals and triumphs might very easily have once been his own.

Wonderful as they were, my father and mother, like most parents of those days (and often today) made the grave error of believing that anyone in authority must be wiser than they. They accepted as irrefutable every thought and idea expressed by my teachers—even misguided ones—and this frequently led to barriers of injustice and resentment.

We must all of us have experienced those youthful conflicts when we felt a great need to be understood—times when we sought direction and encouraging leads but all too often without finding them. This has ever been the way with minds of every potential. Some of our most inspirational figures were misjudged as being hopelessly inadequate by their teachers at school. Edison, for one, was sent home with a note advising his mother that it might be as well to remove him to a school for subnormal children. One with such an advanced and naturally creative mind would no doubt find it doubly hard to concentrate on facts which seemed small and of little import to his extended vision.

If we've been intimidated and made to see ourselves as ungifted and rather dull, perhaps we can take consolation. Those "brilliant" people who seem to be so superior may just have photographic brains and a good memory for facts. We might well have the power to reverse that position by bringing out talents too long neglected.

Most of us, it seems, live on the surface of living and are easily swept by every ripple—influenced by all we see, hear, and feel, by situations and social relationships, by the ideas and mental attitudes of the writers of books and television scripts. How many of us truly understand ourselves or know how deep convictions come to be born? We could go on searching and never find the true beginning of a strongly held opinion. Aren't we all hypnotized from the moment we understand the meaning of words and swayed by them as easily as the wind sways a field of tall grass?

All these forces from the world around us unite to create a continual flow of pressure upon ourselves, almost as though the world were exerting hypnotic influences upon our characters. Little by little this pressure works deep into our lives. We begin to lose the courage to think our own thoughts or express our own feelings or opinions. We live more and more in the great pattern of conformities. Whatever others think, we think. Whatever yardsticks are generally accepted, then they become our own measurements and guides also.

Separating illusion from truth is a most difficult exercise for most of us. Our values have become so jostled and chaotic that we hardly know which things matter and which are purely ephemeral. And yet, at times, we have a strong sense of "knowing"—a state we frequently feel in the presence of great beauty or joy, one we often touched as children and which is familiar to us in dreams. In such rare moments of uplift we glimpse ultimate understanding and the answer to all we seek to know. Here, too, perhaps we catch a glance of our real self, a self wonderfully worth knowing and encouraging, a someone who is reaching out and reminding us that we can never be content to live within the cramping walls of conformity or to become the servants of mass-produced ideas and the little human traits of prejudice, bigotry, and fear.

If, then, there were some way to be as one with this elusive self of ours and to have a closer understanding of the best in others, this would surely be a tremendous step towards changing restless dissatisfaction into quietude and self belief.

I suppose we all need to find this harmony of being, especially during times of confusion and stress. But no one, it seems, can bring it to us except we ourselves—not so much by striving hard to gain it, as by just "letting go."

There is one simple method of reaching such serenity, perhaps the only workable method on which we can always rely. That is to develop by daily patient practice the ability to create the state of "stillness" at those moments when we need direction and strength. We can preserve a period each day when we take off the layers of pressure and discard the urgent claims on our thoughts and time—quietly removing them and consciously laying them aside as if they were heavy, constricting clothing. We can relax in some favorite spot, close our eyes, and let go of tension bit by bit, right from the toes up to the top of the head, and allow the gentle, healing power of God to smooth away the ripples of anxiety or pain and just "take over." This wonderful Power, we soon find out, has been there all the time, waiting for us to draw it around us. As I was once privileged to hear a great and beloved teacher explain very simply: "Just settle down to 'sunbathe' in the warmth and quiet and love. Very soon you begin to feel recharged and invisibly guided in your ways and thoughts."

The more we practice this, the more quickly and intuitively we tune in and open ourselves to an eternal flow. There is release from psychic pressures so that we are enabled to quiet the internal forces and master our thoughts and behavior. The answer to many a problem and heartbreak will be clearly shown. As understanding grows, we can let go of painful memories and personal frustrations. In other words, we learn to integrate our own resources and are better able to sieve the good from the forces which move in upon us, and so steer our lives and help the lives of our loved ones in the way they most need it.

We all want love more than anything else on earth, and we all want to express love in its truest and most beautiful form. And yet, even with the deepest warmth of feeling, so often the results fall short of our expectations. Perhaps because we need understanding and reassurance so much ourselves, we fail to realize that our dear ones are looking to us to give them the very same thing. When we are chosen to be the one entrusted to share the innermost needs and hopes of another human being, whether as wife, husband, or child, it is surely the ultimate in compliments and faith. And by finding out about the other's needs and dreams and making them our own, we, too, may also find fulfillment and joy.

So much is said today about youth "taking over" and young people being made to feel far too important. In certain groups of society, children do seem to be given a dangerous amount of latitude before they are mature enough to handle it. Some parents are unprepared, or unable, to give enough of themselves, and leave a great part of their job to outsiders. Others have acquired the belief that, unless permitted to do everything they desire, their youngsters will become frustrated and repressed. But by far the majority just take the easy way out and allow adolescent cunning to overrule their own deep-rooted principles and responsibilities. If accused of being "squares," old-fashioned, or different from other parents, they become confused as to the stand they should take.

The affection of parents is the same as it ever was, and their greatest wish is to give their children every chance to succeed. All too often "giving" is mistaken for "giving in to" and they try to supply their child's needs by gifts and over-leniency. A youngster who is spoiled and uncontrolled is no happier for having his own way. He develops a sense of insecurity and lack of direction. The amount of attention and emphasis given to the teen-age group is one of the abnormalities of this age. These adolescents are made to feel they reign supreme in a world built just around them—a world they are not always wise enough to run.

The teen-agers I have known possessed just as fine, if not finer, qualities than those of their predecessors, though most of them, I must admit, were influenced by athletic objectives. With a healthy young athlete growing up in your home many problems and complexes will take care of themselves. With an absorbing and natural outlet for energies and emotions, a youngster will be too intent on an active goal of his own to seek the stimulation of less wholesome activities. What is more, he will be acquiring self-discipline and self-control.

By enrolling the services of sport as an additional educator we found little need for concern over such things as psychological disturbances. We were fortunate, too, in the understanding and co-operation of Murray's teachers at school, who generously acknowledged that championship sport nurtured qualities above and beyond those achieved in their own sphere alone.

"I am always amazed at the modest way Murray returns to school after one of his record-breaking trips," said one of these masters.

"The newspapers having featured his performances day after day, little boys naturally gather at the school gates hoping for an autograph from him and maybe a word or two of encouragement. Murray walks quietly in and almost seems embarrassed and surprised at so much attention and fuss. This to me is his greatest strength and charm."

This attribute applies to almost any champion I have met. It is awareness of their own limitations that makes them strive that much harder. They know that many factors beyond their own efforts have helped in their achievements. One thought of self-satisfaction, one small slackening of effort, and they could so easily topple from the tiny space at the top.

"Man was made for conflict, not for rest," wrote Emerson. "In action is his power; not in his goals but in his transitions man is great. Instantly he is dwarfed by self-indulgence. The truest state of mind rested in becomes false."

## CHAPTER 10

# CHAMPION IN THE HOUSE

"I wouldn't wish a swimming champion onto my worst enemy," came the startling confession of a well-known coach. It was a sparkling, surf-filled morning, many years ago, and we were sitting with this gentleman watching the progress of the weekly training session at Bondi Club. Being newcomers to the world of swimming, and even greener in our experience of champions, we were puzzled by the vehemence of this strange remark, to say the least.

We looked down at our seven-year-old son, who was taking part in his first competitive races and smiling up at us from time to time, aware that we shared it all with him. "I mean it," continued our friend, "there is no more grueling, heart-testing sport than championship swimming—or perhaps it's just that I'm too soft to be a good coach. Certainly, I go through every hard, anxious minute with my kids. And make no mistake, the training grind that top swimmers must do to stay on top, year in and year out, makes the labors of Hercules look like a jaunt in the sun. It isn't easy to stand by and see them sweating it out, with every muscle aching, or in freezing water and blue with cold, even keeping it up during bouts of sickness. And after all that, only *one* can win. But I've not even started to tell you all that it entails—who knows, one day you might understand yourselves . . ."

There have indeed been times when we have remembered his words and wondered if perhaps he was right after all. But then, it's all in the point of view—and "overcoming" in the end is surely something well worth wishing onto anybody. We acquire the strength of that we overcome.

There is light and shade in every home, but with a champion in the house, emotions are no doubt stretched over a wider range of feelings. One moves from extremes of apprehension and worry, to moments of overwhelming joy and gratitude. Through it all parents must be acutely conscious of the heavy load placed upon a youngster from a very early age. One hopes and tries to lift it, though, paradoxically, one has been partly instrumental in bringing it about. At least one attempts to channel all the effort, the inevitable hurts and disappointments, as well as the triumphs and glory so that they benefit the whole life pattern—and are thus transmuted into character and growth.

It would be grossly misguiding to pretend that bringing up a champion does not greatly affect the home life. Since the crack of the gun, over fourteen years ago, sent Murray streaking on his way to his first big championship win, there's been little chance of calm reflection. But now that our mental stop watch has ceased its impatient ticking, we are able to take stock and perhaps more calmly answer some of the many questions that have been put to us over the years.

It would be expecting the impossible to think that any young "top-liner" could plan, and stick to a rigorous, disciplined timetable, if those around him did not also toe-the-line, and live healthy, disciplined lives as well.

Regular habits of eating and sleeping are essentials, and of course a well-balanced, intelligently planned diet is a constant factor. Social activities must fit into the daily regime. During peak periods at least, the whole family must work and think as one, each with a separate part to play.

There was one family we knew very well, in which there were several children younger than the one who became a well-known champion. The mother expressed great concern when she found that more and more time—and thought—had to be given to her older son as he reached the top ranks. She felt that the other children were missing out on their full share of attention, and that the constant demands of championship sport disorganized their home life. Yet these little brothers and sisters were the ones who felt the greatest joy and pride in the feats of their big brother hero—and were inspired to personal achievement because of it. A family is a unit—and that which comes to one touches all.

In retrospect we tend to remember only the good and wonderful things, which perhaps is as it should be, for the essence extracted from experience is the only lasting worth. The worries, the heartaches and anxieties, which are always a part of human endeavor, might just as well be left behind. They become too heavy a burden if we carry them all around with us for good.

However, for those who see championship material in a youngster, and may be wondering what this may incur, we have tabulated a sort of Gains and Loss Chart, which might affect the home.

*Those things we might have missed in our lives.*

There was less time, or chance, to indulge the everyday, warm experience of home life.

There was a danger of our becoming too coldly machinelike with the demandingly strict timetable which we found essential to the over-all result.

Social activities had to be curtailed, or at least limited. Not only because of the strictly planned regime, but also through the necessity of adhering to the diet we deemed important.

There were periods of extreme apprehension and worry, for

mishaps and illness assume very great proportions when a champion is expected to win and break records every time he competes.

At times, all forces have to be channeled into one medium of expression, while other important potentials must await their development until the appropriate period.

Amateur sport, as well as all amateur pursuits, is a great drain on the pocketbook, if we choose to follow it through to the ultimate.

*The gains and rewards that compensated us.*

A goal, which we thought very worthwhile, brought a meaning into our lives. It kept the mind active, alert, and constantly striving.

There was precious little time to be frittered away on idle or unrewarding pastimes.

A family comes close together when there is a shared and important objective.

By trying to follow the natural laws, and experiencing many hours of training in the fresh air, sunshine, and water, a youngster comes to know, and be wonderfully benefited by, the unlimited forces of nature.

A high standard of physique and personal appearance is attained.

When one reaches the level of championship sport, unending and unique opportunities are opened up.

The disciplined life and the unusual experiences develops the character and personality to its full potential.

The co-ordination of mind and body results in a mental, as well as a physical, adroitness.

Being constantly before the public, as well as having to communicate through world-wide mediums of radio and television, develops confidence, and ease of manner in all social contacts.

Finally, there is an inner joy and satisfaction in having striven for and found that a set goal *can* be reached.

Most spectators awaiting the thrill of a close finish merely see the champions mount their blocks, all ready to win or break a record. Little do they realize how much thought and care has gone into putting them there. If you do embark upon an athletic goal with your young offspring, you will, without doubt, be called upon to fulfill many roles. For instance you'll need to be something of a philosopher in order to bring a meaning to the job you're doing, and to keep an ideal worth striving for. Your knowledge of psychology will be put to good use in maintaining an optimistic interest in the face, and distress, of inevitable defeat, and in encouraging, at all times, the right frame of mind to bring out maximum effort. A working knowledge of diet is an obvious essential. Any experience of physiotherapy and massage will prove to be invaluable in relaxing tension during periods of strain. This is an asset, too, in stimulating muscles into top condition, and in bringing a feeling of well-being before a race.

Our enthusiasm and interest in Murray's progress had a wonderful boomerang effect in our own lives. For instance, mainly for reasons of example and encouragement we began a before-breakfast swim habit when Murray was very young. This brought enjoyment and a gloriously fit, alive feeling which we'd never known before. I'm sure the neighbors thought us a little crazy to be running around in swim suits on winter mornings while they hugged the fire and warmed themselves with cups of hot coffee. Actually we came to really look forward to that daily tune-up. The sting of cold water made every cell glow and seemed to insulate us against the chilliest weather, while the winter colds we'd accepted as normal gradually became a rare event.

There was something, too, in the early freshness of the gardens surrounding our pool which reinforced the spirit and helped one through the pressures of the coming day.

The results of this regime must have become outwardly apparent, for parents began asking if we would take on the training of their children as well. But this is such a very personal responsibility needing—in the early stages any-way—a close relationship and twenty-four hours a day on the job. The parents themselves were the ones who could have brought about the change had they sincerely wished to do so.

How far-reaching are the influences of our beginnings! The conditions which first mold us, the personalities who first influence our thinking, these can start the whole design of our lives. The seed which comes implanted in every new life has a strong and glorious tree already built within it. It is up to us parents to tend its growth. There are individual strengths and qualities waiting to unfold, human weaknesses to be supplanted.

We have all long outgrown the old idea that we own our little ones or have any right to shape them to our will. We know them to be separate individuals, come to us for aid in the groundwork. But while that job lasts, it is just about the biggest and most far-reaching one we'll ever be called upon to perform. When we remember that the whole of the future generation, its aims, its values, the way in which it runs the world, depends on the unfoldment of each equally vital individual, the all-encompassing mission of our task is fully brought home.

There is surely a divinely planned idea behind a true home and the timeless Mother-Father principle which sustains it. The Mother symbol has always stood for love, patience, sacrifice, and inspiration, while the Father symbol brings meaning to these qualities and gives them strength and form. From the time she captured the promise hidden in every fairy tale, Mother has been building her dreams. Father, who must give so much of himself to the practical job of earning a living, often loses sight of the fact that he brought that dream to life. An unexpected gift of flowers can bring immeasurable joy, and a word of tender assurance encourages her as nothing else can in a sometimes over-demanding job.

On the other hand, we mothers can become so immersed in the habitual daily round that we are apt to forget the person whom our husbands married and even become careless of the very qualities he most loved. He may know of her gratitude and admiration, but it's only human to need such thoughts constantly bolstered by words and actions.

As I look back, I realize how wonderfully Ian has fulfilled his role of father. His co-operation, love, and sympathetic understanding have been an essential part of any success. First and last, Ian has been the brains, the student engaged in an inexhaustible search for knowledge and truth. *He* put in the groundwork which made our way easier. He kept us supplied with everything we needed, no matter where we might be. And, far too often, he was the generous-hearted "swimming widower."

I suspect that the thought of having an athletic son was the last thing that ever entered his mind. Never robust, even bordering on the delicate when young, his interests were always of an intellectual nature. The idea of being the father of a famous world champion would have once seemed an impossible fantasy.

He would smile on our first efforts. "You have the faith," he used to say, "and Murray the guts to train miles every day. Far be it for me not to encourage you both in every way that I can."

Years later, when he spent overtime at the office answering a world-wide fan mail requesting answers to problems—ranging from those of gravely disturbed delinquents to the best means of encouraging a timid family pet into the water, he knew he had a champion well and truly in the home.

Ian has been the bulwark of our castle in the air and spared nothing of himself in the building of sound foundations.

There are as many books as "authoritative" opinions on how best to handle each phase and facet of child rearing, and I would not presume to attempt any professional instruction. However, I firmly believe that an inborn wisdom comes along in the same package with a newly arrived infant. When we lean upon outsiders to map out our behavior, we inevitably run into trouble. There is no excuse for ignorance, nor for nursing a feeling of inadequacy. These only lead to our domination by those who artfully impress us and so frequently override our own natural intuition.

Intuition is invariably the way through which the best answers come to us. The more we turn to that inner voice, the more clearly comprehensive the message becomes—although being human, we do not always follow it.

It is perhaps harder today than at any other time in history for us to live as we all want to live—simple, healthy, happy, loving lives. When the same dynamic warning is coming from every side, it is surely time for us to do a little self-searching. When experienced and perceptive publicists, lecturers from varying fields of thought, and teachers of spiritual truths are set upon waking us all up before it's too late, then we know the warning to be of a serious nature. We would indeed be living in a fantasy of our own if we didn't recognize the confusion and, in many ways, the deterioration of our standards of behavior.

In a recent address to fellow publicists, a well-known editor, Jenkin Lloyd Jones, of the Tulsa (Oklahoma) *Tribune*, administered some verbal shock treatment. He said:

I don't know how long Americans can stand this erosion of principle. . . . Can anyone deny that movies are dirtier than ever? But they don't call it dirt. They call it "realism." Why do we let them fool us? Why do we nod owlishly when they tell us that filth is merely a daring art form, and licentiousness is really social comment? . . . We are drowning our youngsters in violence, cynicism and sadism piped into the living room and even the nursery. The grandchildren of the kids who used to weep because The Little Match Girl froze to death now feel cheated if she isn't slugged, raped and thrown into a Bessemer converter. . . . Don Maxwell of the Chicago Tribune has recently asked his book department to quit advertising scatological literature by including it in the list of best sellers. The critics and the book publishers have denounced him for tampering with the facts. I would like to raise a somewhat larger question: Who is tampering with the soul of America? For nations do have souls. . . .

Let there be a fresh breeze, a breeze of new honesty, new idealism, new integrity. . . . Let's cover up the cesspool and start planting some flowers. . . .

Have parents ever stopped planting flowers? I am very sure they haven't—and never will, although when they see them struggling to grow and being damaged by the influences of power-and-money-hungry individuals and concerns, they become dispirited about the results of their work. But when the roots have taken a firm enough hold, a plant goes on thriving anyway.

Being above all things a parent, I look to world-wide parenthood for strength and hope in these times of challenge and war on the very spirit of right, and good, and freedom.

Thoughtful parents everywhere are disturbed, and rightly so, that they can no longer count on the educational system to strengthen the principles of good home training. Their children are getting less and less ethical instruction,

less and less disciplined guidance, and less and less of a
wholesome, building diet of homework to help fortify them
against the hypnosis of TV.

Isn't it long past time that we parents firmly took hold
of the reins once again! We, who have allowed the new un-
disciplined way of things to creep into our homes, aren't
we doing a great disservice to this generation? Aren't we
becoming careless of that gift left to us by the mettlesome,
God-fearing pioneers—our way of life?

Is it because we choose to pursue a comfortable, easygoing life ourselves, or because the brainwashing propa-
ganda of "educators" and public "servants" have taken
over the job that is our personal responsibility? Teaching
our children the once unquestioned benefits of discipline,
and indoctrinating them with spiritual and ethical values,
is the greatest protection, the strongest weapon we can give
them to combat an uncongenial world, and the confusion
of lost or distorted values.

It is during that pre-school conditioning period that
seeds of worth and wisdom can be so firmly implanted that
later influences will never be able to completely choke
them back.

When we were quietly bringing up our son on the sun-
drenched beaches of Australia, these brainwashing, under-
mining tactics had not reached our world—or, if they had,
we were blissfully unaware of them. Our world of striving
young champions and their enthusiastically dedicated families brought us into touch with a very different set of challenges and problems, but far-reaching perhaps in their human context.

Sport is by no means all handshakes and heroes. It has
its tedium of daily monotony, its periods of discouragement,
as well as its areas where human weakness and keyed-up
emotions take over. One of the more unfortunate aspects of
sport, or of any competitive field, is that of intense enthusi-

asm turning into something a little fiercer than mere friendly rivalry. It can end in real animosity.

This, of course, can be the misguided outcome of any form of contest. We find it, for instance, in the intensely competitive field of political campaigning where the constant verbal clashes and schemes directed at overthrowing an opponent, can lead to an antagonism amounting to a real hate-complex. But anything of so disturbing a nature rarely happens in true amateur sport. In fact, the healthy, vibrant competitive spirit wonderfully strengthens the character as well as the body. It is important, nevertheless, to hold fast to the higher aims of self-mastery and to concentrate on perfection of technique rather than just the will to beat the other fellow.

In our own experience we found that a wonderful sympathy existed between swimmers at all times. If there were any misdirected feelings then it could only have been among the lookers-on. I do recall being told of a certain father who became so emotionally stirred that he actually struck his champion-son when he didn't get the better of his opponents in a race. Such zeal can express itself in strange forms, but surely these are rare and isolated cases. Personally, we found nothing but the highest ideals of sportsmanship existing in amateur athletics.

We are told that man is basically governed by two emotions: that of fear—and that of love. One leads to confusion, animosity, and misery; the other to quietude and successful fulfillment. And so it is through any medium which absorbs our energies at various stages of our development.

One of the most spirited "horses" an athlete must learn to handle is that of natural human emotion. A certain athletic coach, dedicated as all good coaches are, asked me to bring up this simple, everyday hazard with its power to snatch away goals at the very moment of their fulfillment.

"Please put would-be champions on their guard," he said. "Intense emotional attachments with their distractions have been the means of many a name disappearing from the headlines. They can be the bane and heartbreak of both hard-working coaches and dedicated athletes alike."

He was not alluding, I feel sure, to the sympathetic understanding of real love, which surely brings added inspiration and extra determination to succeed, but to the more ephemeral, though often intensely demanding association, which can dissipate so much valuable thought and time.

Just a short time ago, I was approached by the sister of a young champion. "My brother is just reaching the top," she said, "he has proved himself as a state and national champion, and has every opportunity of making the next Olympic Games. Of course, the family has done everything to help him since he first started. Now he has a girl friend who expects him to be with her every night. Consequently, he's cutting his training, eating in snack bars and becoming careless about his diet, and rapidly losing his form and all chances of attaining the goal he has worked so hard to reach. Is there anything we can do to bring him back to his senses—and help him to the success he deserves?"

What advice is there to give? Out of the millions of athletes in the world, how few of them ever make the Olympics or famed renown. Such laurels are not easily won. Surely, the athlete himself must know where he is heading, and how much he is prepared to give in overcoming the obstacles between himself and his goals. It can be done, but only the champion himself can make those last difficult steps.

Sharing children's hurts is made no easier for knowing them to be a necessary part of becoming adult. Such growing pains, in our case, usually came through sport. I never forget how keenly we felt during the first thrilling promise of an overseas tour.

One day Murray rushed home, tremendously excited, and told us: "I have been invited on a swimming tour of New Zealand with Thiele" (the Queensland Backstroke Champion). The boys were very happy and keen to go. It did seem some little reward for the hard work they had given to their sport. The really big thrill was having the honor of representing their country, and so becoming eligible to wear the green blazer with Australia's coat-of-arms on the pocket, the most coveted garment of any Aussie sportsman. A special order for making this was being rushed through. We also started inquiries as to the availability of health foods.

It was the time of the State Championships, and on the night that Murray was about to mount his block for the 440-yard title race, an official with complete absence of thought, told him that the New Zealand trip had been arbitrarily canceled! It seemed that New Zealand officials thought that Murray was not well known enough to draw a "big gate."

The need for so great a disappointment was proved to be quite unnecessary—a short time later Murray made his first world record, and hundreds of disappointed spectators had to be turned away from Sydney's Olympic pool. The following year this tour did eventuate when the New Zealand Swimming Association again invited Murray and, this time, Jon Henricks, the world sprint champion to visit their island of the "Long White Cloud." The boys were given a tremendous welcome wherever they appeared and will always remember the kind hospitality that was shown to them. However, after a year of excitement, triumphs and growing up, the great thrill of that first boyish adventure had lost much of its magic.

And we parents who must constantly draw from our store

of patience, strength, and wise counsel—where can we go to recharge our own batteries when they run down? No doubt we each have our private source of inspiration, whether it be from the teachings of a religion which is a part of us; the profundity of some age-old master or the transcendent thoughts we catch from our own little garden. It is the same voice we hear, the same understanding answer to our particular need.

Each individual must find for himself the way which most suits his own nature. The need and desire to do so is all that counts. Surely there is something in this reaching out to glimpse infinities that can be caught and brought back through the brush of a fine artist or through the notes of a superb musician—and, yes, even through the striving of a great athlete.

## CHAPTER 11

## ON THE SIDELINES

*"'Tis a great vice in all countries, the sacrifice of heroes to be courtiers and diners-out, to talk for the amusement of those who wish to be amused . . . What with egotism on one side and levity on the other, we shall have no Olympus."*

Emerson

Sometimes we would answer our phone to hear a strange voice say, "We don't know Murray, but we're giving a big party tonight, and our guests would be most interested to meet him." Of course they couldn't have known that our son had just completed ten miles of strenuous training and now faced several hours of study for tomorrow's math exam, plus an early-morning rise for further swimming conditioning. Being in the public eye at an early age can bring its problems along with its flattering attentions. So many kindly, well-meaning people wish to extend their hospitality to any headline personalities. When it is pointed out that late nights and smoky rooms could mean the loss of a race, or at best, reduce the time of an important record attempt, they are usually quick to understand.

Being sociable is one thing! But social life for its own sake can be a most destructive energy-waster. Our young athletes may need a little directing until they are mature enough to discriminate for themselves, which, when they realize the full implications, they quickly do.

There may have been times when we appeared over-anxious and too demanding, as most parents will. This rarely stems from any desire of assuming parental dictatorship, but rather from an innate wish to steer them away from likely disappointment and to assure their happy fulfillment. The day must come when our youngsters see us as just people and not models of infallibility and acquire an understanding tolerance for our human make-up. There is then a sounder basis for a worthwhile friendship. True friendship, it has been aptly said, "is not formed of glass threads or frost work but the solidest thing we know." Our friends are deeply interwoven into the pattern of our lives, and we are especially aware of the varying effects of "friends" in the lives of our children. They can do so much to encourage the finest within them, or help to dissipate their potential by bringing out the lazy acceptance of this amusement-ridden world. We have all experienced at one time or another how misdirected energies have been wonderfully rechanneled through the enthusiasm of a friend; how perhaps the shared and stimulating interest of a pal has helped to uncover a youngster's talent on the football field, or a natural aptitude for aeronautics. Maybe your little girl is of a sensitively philosophical nature, like the one whose home I frequently visit. I remember her running to her mother and saying, "Anne thinks that God's thoughts make the flowers grow and that's why we all love them so much."

She had found a friend with whom she could exchange ideas and so encourage the growth of a sweet and searching mind.

A young champion has a special need for the right kind of friends. Having to live to a rather austere pattern, to give up many of the lighter pleasures for continuous hard work, he must have the balancing effect of warm, understanding companions. The sort of pals who share his goal with him, and yet treat him as a sociable human being and not just a racing machine.

Most of Murray's own pals lived the same out-of-door life that he did. When races were over, they would chase up the two miles of white Bondi sand, or shoot the powerful rolling breakers as they swept in from the Pacific. He was fortunate in being able to spend sunny leisure hours with such companions. As is the way of boys, they shared a camaraderie and a private world of jokes and fun. There was of course one close friend who shared a little more than all the rest. A co-prefect at a school and a dedicated member of the swimming team, he and Murray found deeper things in common as well as the other ephemeral world of surf and sport and strong, sun-tanned limbs. Though they have been oceans and years apart, this "something" may prove to be that rare blessing of lifelong friendship.

The tremendous competition of racing against such friends, week in and week out, and year after year, their loyal belief and lusty support at every championship and record-making swim, can never be underestimated as a very great contribution to final success.

When a coach comes into the life of a champion's babyhood days, he more than earns the title of friend. During those years when Murray was evolving into a swimming star, these two were so closely linked that it became impossible to think of Murray without Sam Herford, or of Sam without Murray. This tie of athlete and coach is the spark which lights up every history-making story of sport. Sam will always be a figure in the forefront of Murray's swimming life, and I am sure that it was no mere chance that brought him onto our little beach during Murray's dog-paddling days. And what of Sam himself? Sun, wind, and sea are deep in every pore of his being, giving the impression of hard, bronzed toughness. So often has he had to throw his voice across the splashing of water and the shouting of children that it has become naturally amplified and resounds through any clamor—always to find its mark. For all his outer bluntness his heart is gentle and warm—and we had every chance to know, for he would give his all to "Mu" (his affectionate shortening of Murray's name) whenever the need arose.

During the school semester, when it was impossible for Murray to go to him, he would willingly get up at 5 A.M. and drive the twelve miles to our pool in order to supervise Murray's training before school lessons began. On the occasions when Murray had to attend some far-off swimming event he never hesitated to leave his family and his business at the baths. He would always be there with his advice and support, making sure that this young champ of his was well cared for and at his best. But if any of Sam's charges were caught loafing or not playing the game, then all hell would be let loose.

He was well prepared—and very accustomed to the inevitable excuses before every big event. "I've drawn John in the first heat. He's right in the groove and will leave me for dead!" or "Garry has done miles more training than I have—I haven't a chance!" In these cases of jitters and lack of confidence he knew exactly how to administer a strong dose of his own snap-out-of-it medicine. If a swimmer were ill, tense—or had some real cause for anxiety—then he would be ready with all the sympathy and understanding in the world.

"My system, tried and proved over the years, is to obtain a congenial training atmosphere—make the kids work together and mix fun with the serious side of their training." That was Sam's philosophy.

He trained swimmers to suit their own personalities. During their early years, when every other Australian champion was swimming up to ten miles a day, Murray was making records on a daily schedule of far less mileage.

"I'll let Murray turn seventeen before I'll train him seriously," said Sam. "Too many swimmers have been burnt out by being sent against the clock in their early teens. When I decide to send Murray Rose, most of his contemporary swimmers will get the surprise of their lives. Murray will be at his top for the Olympic Games. Then, he will defeat the rest of the world."

In every one of his forecasts Sam was dead right. So accurate was he in these prophecies that he was able to predict the exact time, often to within a tenth of a second, in which Murray would win a race. And he would do this some months before the race took place. It was as though Murray had a stop watch built into his brain which synchronized with the one Sam held in his hand. Sam's tremendous force, determination, and unshakable faith brought an ever ready recharge of strength, not only to Murray but often to me, when I gave way to doubts and anxiety. Most of Murray's preparation—in fact a great deal of his early life—was put in at Sam Herford's baths. Here he worked alongside yet a further group of friends, those who shared the aches of tedious training hours. These were vigorous, joyful days that only youth could sustain and which, I feel sure, none of them will ever forget.

While we are here in this typical Australian setting, let us take a look at Sam's Swim School, and join in some of the day's activities. The quiet beauty of Sydney harbor is seen on every side. The sun, catching the white sails of passing yachts and pouring its warmth onto the training pool, promises a pleasant day for the scheduled swimming program.

Part of the pool is roped off into lanes and reserved for the exclusive use of serious swimmers, those boys and girls with important championships ahead who have dreams of winning titles, breaking records, or just gaining a place. So tough is the competition in Australian swimming, that even to be sure of reaching a final, many hours of grueling work are essential.

Murray's daily trip from our home on the other side of the harbor would take around one hour and a half by tram and bus and train. Imagine him arriving, swinging the inevitable swimmers' bag always bulging with towels, swim trunks, pullovers, sweat suits, and lunch. He joins the row of brown bodies stretched out in the morning sun, soaking in the last lazy moments before Sam appears to put them to work.

The first part of the training is usually several miles of relaxed swimming to build up stamina and condition. Sometimes the monotony of the everlasting up-and-down grind would be relieved by swimming with arms alone while the feet are held together by a thick rubber band. This developed strong shoulders and dorsal muscles and gave power to the pull under the water, unseen by the spectators, but the answer to many a spectacular win. There would also be periods with hands stretched out in front on a cork kicking board in order to strengthen legs and thighs and make the ankles more flexible.

Sam would be keenly observing any little faults and calling continuously to one or the other, "Keep that head down," "Pull more with the left," "Don't stiffen up—relax, relax!"

Several hours of this and one by one they would finish their allotted distance and climb out for a well-earned rest and lunch.

While tired bodies untensed, they might relax to music, play chess or cards, and fall asleep for a time. Sam's voice would shake them back, and the afternoon session began. If the championships were close there would be windsprints, hard 50-meter laps with thirty seconds' rest between them.

It was Murray's custom to swim up to nine fast quarter-

Peter Daland—Murray's famous coach in America. *(Photo by Phil Bath for* Sports Illustrated)

The training grind, year in and year out, made the labors of Hercules look like a stroll in the sun.

At Townsville, "our" team of young athletes set about their training with all the keenness of the idyllic youth of Greece centuries before. From left: Jon Henricks, Dawn Fraser, Gary Chapman, Murray, Lorraine Crapp, David Thiele. (*Sydney* Morning Herald *photo*)

The best medicine to full recovery was a world-record swim. (*Sydney* Morning Herald *photo*)

Four Aussie Olympic gold medalists during training period at Townsville pool. From left: John Konrads, Murray, John Devitt, Jon Henricks. (*Photo by Australian Consolidated Press Ltd., Sydney*)

After a week of grueling championships a tired hero finds himself still on the job. At the British Empire Games in Perth, Murray won four gold medals for Australia. (*Photo by Australian Consolidated Press Ltd., Sydney*)

Murray and Yamanaka of Japan. Though meeting on an intensively competitive ground, there is warm camaraderie in the Olympic Games. (*Sydney* Morning Herald *photo*)

I hoped that something of the message of this day would stay with us always. The Australian team enters the arena at Melbourne. (*Photo by Ken Rainsbury, Melbourne*)

There were messages from friends we knew — and many, many more from those we'd never met. *(Photo by Australian Consolidated Press Ltd., Sydney)*

This is the moment they have trained for, month after month, hour after weary hour. *(Photo by Frank Mullins)*

I pictured the thousands who would be tuned in to this spot at this moment as the swimmers awaited the starter's call. *(Photo by Marvin E. Newman for* Sports Illustrated*)*

Our golden finish—the last race in the Melbourne Games. *(Photo from the* Herald-Sun, *Melbourne)*

This was a moment of pure gold and one that I have locked away in my heart. After the epic 1500-meter struggle in Melbourne. Place-getters were Yamanaka of Japan and Breen of the United States. (*Sydney Morning Herald photo*)

Murray off to talk about the races he might have won. The team of NBC commentators about to leave Los Angeles for the Olympic Games in Tokyo. From left to right: Bud Palmer, Rafer Johnson (America's decathlon champion of the Melbourne and Rome Olympics), Jim Simpson, Bill Henry, and Murray.

There is no end—only new beginnings. (*Sydney* Morning Herald *photo*)

mile time trials per day at this stage, each one faster than its predecessor if possible. At other times, fast starts and turns would be practiced many times over. Patience, determination, hard work—all this and more—that is where medals begin to be a fact.

As the sun starts leaving the pool, a day of training comes to an end. Now the youngsters can think of games and they noisily clown as they prepare to go home. Appetites need no stimulus; their enjoyment of the waiting meal is assured; then, nine or ten hours of the sort of sleep that refreshes and rebuilds for another day.

It was fortunate that Sam so utterly believed in our natural way of life and was happy to leave the home conditioning almost entirely to us. We had no wish to encroach on each other's territory and learned to act and put our faith in the other's part.

"Give him the full works, mum!" were his only instructions before a big event, "we must have him at his top on Saturday!" By this, he meant especial attention to well-balanced meals and every "extra" stamina-giving food. He meant a quiet background and plenty of sleep and the vitamin intake for "racing" days. He meant massage to induce a relaxing sleep before the race and another on awakening to stimulate the muscles. And, if it was to be a long or hard battle, some extra time on important muscles with a penetrating oil to combat the likelihood of aches, pains, stiffness, or cramps. Most of all, he meant a constant flow of cheerful, positive thoughts and the unperturbed belief of love. That was the formula he endorsed.

It is fitting that Sam, who gave his all to Murray, should have been nominated as Swimming Coach of the Year—largely, he stated, as a result of the successes of his first world champ and lifelong friend. It was doubly gratifying when a few years later Peter Daland, Murray's equally great coach in America, received the same recognition.

Why do such achievements mean so much? What makes us work so hard, and so long, in the cause of sport? Is there true justification for such dedicated absorption? The answer, which most likely echoes from every sportsman's heart, has been the inspiration behind the words of Arnold Kaech, director of the Swiss School of Sport and Gymnastics:

. . . While we are engaged in sport we move in the blessed realm of childhood; while we are engaged in sport the dreams of youth are still alive within us. We give freely of ourselves because we ask nothing in return. When we engage in sport we are at play; and it is only at play *that man is truly man,* so Schiller has told us. To many, this play seems an activity of the body merely. They see the body in movement, the vigor of a stroke, the swing of a gymnast's arms and legs, but they do not see what goes on inside. They do not see all—it is as if a man should look at a picture and see nothing but lines and colors, or read a score and never hear the music. The body and the feats it performs, are ends to them, whereas in true sport the performance is not an end in itself—nor the body either—but the means of expression. Moving over the ground, thrusting through the water, gliding over the snowy slopes, or wrestling with the rock-face—these are expressions of the joy of life itself, expressions of the well-being won from living close to nature. The body is but the means of expression, the instrument the soul requires to enable it to measure the territory which has been granted to man, and occupy it to the limit.

Only thus can we explain why "they which run in a race run all, but one receiveth the prize", only thus understand how records can go on for ever being broken, at the cost of suffering, of sacrifice, and even of the total dedication of life itself. Sport is the faithful image of the struggle of humanity towards perfection; in sport soul and body together strive to accomplish the age-old aspiration of mankind—"faster, harder, higher."

There lies "the point" of sport, its whole importance, its true meaning. It needs no further justification.

## CHAPTER 12

## OBSTACLES AND THE OLYMPICS

Two years before the Melbourne Games saw us making preparations for our part in them. Presumptuous? Perhaps. But was ever anything gained by being half-hearted? Murray, at that time, could not have found the food to which he was accustomed in the Australian team's commissary. It would be imperative, therefore, for us to establish a base from which we could provide a power-packed diet when necessary.

With this in mind, we took several flights to the future site of the Olympics. We walked many miles around the rough wasteland out of which was to grow the most modern Olympic Village yet to be seen. Surrounding it, there sprawled a suburb of small private homes with no apartments to be rented—and no one, it seemed, would even consider any propositions for leasing a house.

We spent hours making inquiries and knocking on doors until at last we met some young newly marrieds with an up-to-date villa about two miles from the site of the future Village. Luckily for us, they were keen sports enthusiasts and had been following Murray's efforts from the very beginning of his sports career. After we had explained the reasons for our now weary searching and offered the highest rent we could possibly afford, they finally agreed to sign over their home for six weeks, the period of the team's stay in Melbourne.

Murray, a fifteen-year-old schoolboy at that time, had his heart set on the big event still many months away. Making the team for the Games would mean an all-out effort for him as well as taking time off from school during that important year. He was therefore studying especially hard and taking extra tuition in the vacation periods. Educationally, he must be prepared for any eventuality which might cut into his school semester.

Prospective representatives were chosen from each sport based on their performances in the championships prior to the Games. From these trial squads the final Olympic team would be chosen. Murray was selected to join the swimming squad whose members faced a training grind more intensive than any before. Each chosen youngster was understandably proud and willing to endure the most rigorous discipline which might earn him a coveted place of honor.

It is well-known now that this Australian swimming team of 1956 became world-renowned for its prowess in the water. What lay behind the acclaim they won? Was there a secret back of their success? Officials and coaches from other countries were deeply interested in their method of training. Always on the lookout for improved ideas, they were anxious to get the full story.

For that story we must go back to the babyhood of those champions. In a large part of Australia, where summer lasts most of the year, an athlete is encouraged to give everything he has to conditioning and training before all else. Rightly or wrongly the call of the beach, the tennis court, the golf course, and the cricket oval tends to take precedence over most other things. This worship of sport is inborn in the nature of Australians, and every chance possible is given to a sportsman, or sports child, who shows real promise.

The thousands of miles of enticing white beaches, the warm, rolling surf and sunny rock pools hold all the elements needed for producing wizards in the water. Almost before they can walk, children are encouraged to swim, and are given expert coaching whenever they excel. Growing up in such a background one might well expect to find the greatest reserve of talent in the swimming world.

"Our" team started their Olympic preparation stretch with ten weeks of calisthenics and special land exercises to develop muscles for swimming. Emerging from their training at the Athletic Club in Sydney, these youngsters drew sympathetic smiles from passersby. Wrapped in colored sweaters and wearing bright woolen caps, they walked stiffly and painfully, for every limb protested at the amount of exercise forced upon it. When I unpacked the T shirts Murray wore during a workout, I could wring out the sweat as one wrings a garment after it has been soaking in a tub.

The second stage of conditioning took place in a pool in Townsville, a small town in the tropical belt of Australia, close to the Barrier Reef. This was a perfect spot for winter training, the southern cities now being several overcoats colder. To me, the months in Townsville brought a conflict of emotions. There was the natural pride in Murray's achievements, and the privilege of sharing the efforts of an Olympic team in action. But it also meant my first long parting from Ian, and an unjourneyable distance between me and my home. At the last moment I weakened and questioned the need for going, for a recurrence of pain undermined my resolution. But Ian and my closest friends left me in no doubt whatever that accepting the challenge and finding the courage was the very least expected from the mother of a champion. Had I realized then that the path we had chosen would lead to further and longer partings, I might have found the decision even harder to make. But we are only asked to go one step at a time, and to live each moment as it comes. After years of such decisions, I have never found the answer to the problem of a heart in two places.

Before leaving Sydney four members of the team had appeared on a radio quiz and won free transport for more than twenty of the selected competitors. During part of the time a living allowance was paid to team members by the Australian Swimming Association. For those, like Murray, who, having a different regimen, desired a home base, the money had to be found by parents. Throughout this period we learned the hard way that if you choose to follow an unconventional pattern you must pay for the luxury of nursing such ideals.

When we arrived at our apartment in this leisurely coastal town, we found nothing of the outward sense of quietude there. We received our first shock when we saw, or rather heard, its close proximity to an open-air movie theater. Added to that, the buildings in the tropical North are mostly wooden structures, and because of intense year-round heat, the use of carpets is eliminated. The noise of stamping feet in the apartment above, the gunfire and screams from the theater next door would have made rest impossible during the strenuous weeks ahead—weeks when every ounce of energy would be needed, and each moment of sleep was essential.

In my hunt for a more suitable base I combed the streets of Townsville but with no luck. Returning home fatigued and rather downhearted, I stopped to look in at the pool, which was a good three miles from our present flat. I could hardly believe my eyes, for what I saw was too ideal to be true. Overlooking the sea and adjoining the team's training headquarters, was a vacant bungalow.

"There's just no hope of getting that," the others smiled knowingly when they saw my excitement. "We've all been on their backs for weeks, but the owners are adamant in their refusal to rent it."

Somehow I knew that that was where we would live, and I silently resolved to go after it. Luck was with us. I heard of a business contact living in the town who knew the property and the people who owned it. They were kindly and most understanding, and great swimming enthusiasts as well. Their grandfather, they explained, had left the house suddenly because of a serious illness. As it had stood untouched, and uncleaned for several years they believed it to be quite uninhabitable. Besides, there was the danger of rotting wood, especially on the back veranda. I promised to put the chaos in order, and to avoid any ant-eaten boards, and naturally assured them that care would be given to their personal goods. They could see how much it meant to us, and how grateful we'd be to have it. The key of the door came with the key of their warmly sympathetic hearts.

The abandoned little house was temporarily ours, and I willingly began the task of taking over. Other swimmers' parents and kind Townsville friends generously came to my aid. We cleaned away debris, tore down cobwebs, eliminated the cockroaches who had moved in there, and removed the years' accumulation of dust and grime.

Neighbors brought us blankets and comfortable beds and many useful, homely necessities. The radio was mended, the light and power turned on, and the luxury of the latest electrical gadgets added. Jugs and vases filled with exotic flowers brought the bungalow charmingly to life—and we became the envy of the rest of the team.

"Did you hear a strange noise very early this morning?" Murray asked on our first day. I certainly did. While it was still dark, I also had been awakened by a sound very like the mooing of a calf. It was eerie, disturbing, and persistent. When Murray came home to rest between training sessions the sound began again. Was rest and sleep again to evade us?

It took several days of scouting before we tracked down

its source—a pair of unusually large and lusty pigeons who had built their nest right over a window in Murray's room.

With a long rod I found it just possible to reach the nest, but when I started to pry it loose I found that my heart just couldn't sanction this destruction. Murray felt pretty much the same. "Leave them in peace—I don't mind the noise," was his reaction.

I told Sam of our difficulty, quite expecting him to say: "What nonsense! I'll soon have that out of the way!" I should have known him better. "I wouldn't destroy the nest either," was his reply, "cruelty can never be right."

I ended the trouble by tying a rag onto a long pole and allowing it to flutter near the nest when sleep was necessary. I'm sure the pigeons were not particularly pleased about this disturbance but at least they were able to retain their home and hatch out their young.

In the room where Murray slept, we devised the strangest of decors. Having no drapes for the windows, we hung up dark tablecloths on pieces of string. As the owners' goods filled all of the cupboards and drawers, we tied strong cord onto screws in the walls, and everything he wore or used had to be draped over them. In spite of such odd nonconformities and the exceptional demands during this rigorous training period, the unreality of it all brought its own humor and close companionship. It was also a warmly pleasant time—at least in retrospect.

I especially remember the mornings when, after the early training session, we would sit eating breakfast on the wooden front-door steps, from where we could see the next group of swimmers working out. We became familiar with the daily passersby, identifying them with names we thought appropriate. There was the smartly groomed lawyer who chose to walk to his office along the edge of the sea each day; the schoolboy on his bicycle who wore gay Hawaiian shirts; the faithful shaggy dog who joyously accompanied his master to a certain tree, then turned and, drooping, sadly walked back on his own. And the gentle nuns, whose white faces surprisingly contrasted with the deep tan of most other people. They would quietly come and go through the gates of the nearby convent attempting, at times, to distract their young female pupils from a too deep interest in the physical perfections of Olympic manhood.

As usual, much of our food had to be air-freighted the 1200-odd miles from Sydney. I had been loaned a little portable electric squeezer, with which to make the countless pints of carrot, celery, and pineapple juices that Murray needed to store up natural, energy-giving sugars. There was also a goat farm close at hand from which we obtained new milk, fresh, sweet, and unpasteurized, from animals which grazed on sun-strewn pastures.

Fresh ripe fruit was wonderfully abundant. It grew to amazingly large proportions and had a honeylike, mouthwatering taste.

And so, Murray and this team of young athletes began to set about their training with all the keenness of the idyllic youth of Greece centuries earlier.

Before the mornings were light I would awake to hear the slap, slap, slap of strong muscular arms threading their way through the pool below, lap upon lap, perpetually up and down. The youngsters in the first session were on their way. The early risers had begun the first part of their training schedule of six to ten miles a day. Slow, long miles of conditioning for some; short, fast sprints for others; or turns and take-offs according to the abilities and needs of each individual swimmer. I watched them from my balcony while my own limbs ached in sympathy. Between the workouts they would stretch out on the grass, relaxing and playing poker dice as their bodies "recovered" and built up reserves for further work.

Liners taking holiday-makers on South Sea island cruises included this hard-working training team as one of their "sights" of interest. Bodies became brown and more gloriously fit than ever before. It was a joy to watch their developing strength and rhythmic grace of movement.

The kindly people of Townsville were generous in their acceptance of this invasion. Many opened their homes and took care of the young athletes' needs; others offered comforts and necessities such as laundering clothes and supplying transport. On the rare rest days they were shown the local highlights and bountifully entertained. And for swing-loving swimmers taking time off from the grind, a radio station ran a session of each team member's favorite tunes.

Day after day the tropic sky was brilliant, clear, and blue—but for us the clouds were gathering, and our first time of testing was at hand.

Murray came in one day with ominous signs of cold and fever and was understandably disturbed. "I can't be ill now," he said rather anxiously. "This is far too important a period." But he was. Illness sometimes strikes when an athlete is trained to the peak. Perhaps it was overstrain, since he had never been the really rugged type, or maybe I had been loading him up with too many of the "building" foods. It is often hard to judge the correct food intake when one is over-keen to give every ounce of power. It can be all too easy to become over-zealous and so equip an athlete with excess baggage, even of the very best kind. Murray's temperature started to mount, and he came down with a serious attack of flu. Night after sleepless night his coughing shook the flimsy wooden structure which housed us.

"You'll be all right, fella, the rest will do you good!" Sam tried hard to keep up the fading morale. With a flushed face and a head too heavy to lift, Murray listened to that ceaseless slap, slap coming from the pool outside.

His powerful teammates were getting stronger and

faster, for the Games were now only weeks away. For us, the Olympic flame burned very low just then, one of its several dangerous flickers before it shone out steadily bright again.

At such times there are but two paths. The orthodox way, which leads to suppressive drugs, and the "half-well" weary feeling that such treatments so often leave behind. Or the natural method of cleaning out the toxic bloodstream, longer and more difficult perhaps but surer of results in the end.

Going along with the theory that nature was showing us strongly that poisons had accumulated in the system, we determined to do everything we possibly could to making the body quickly fit again.

For the next few days Murray stopped eating altogether. He just drank pints of freshly squeezed juice from sweetly ripe pineapples. To aid this cleansing process, wet pads were continuously applied to his chest, throat and spine. Constant massage greatly helped during this period, for muscles which had been developed with such mighty physical effort had to be kept as fit and firm as possible. Gradually the poisons ebbed away, strength flowed back, and he began eating solid food. Even so, nature had not completed her job. A large and painful abscess appeared on his thigh, bearing four or five heads. Though it restricted movement and caused intense pain, Murray could spare no further time from training.

"Abscess or not I can't be out of that water another minute," he said. Shaken, and still weak, he got back to his swimming and started catching up on lost time and lost condition.

Intense tropical heat was now bearing down on the bodies moving up and down the pool, and the team manager decided that it was time to move the group to a more temperate zone. The next base was Brisbane in southern

Queensland, where the sunshine was more benign and ideally suited to the swimmers' needs. A temporary exception had to be made for Murray, for the team manager thought it best for him to stay behind until he had regained lost condition and caught up on his full quota of basic training.

When the team climbed aboard the specially chartered DC-6 their sunburned faces were shadowed by wide-brimmed woven palm hats, and as mementos of their stay, most of them carried coconuts painted with brilliant scenes. A large crowd had gathered to send them happily on their way, and quite a few, especially among the girl friends they left behind, had a hard time keeping back the tears.

The middle of the day now being dangerously hot, Murray did most of his lone training around dawn and late at night. On one of those very dark nights, unable to see the end of the unlit pool, he crashed into the tiles and came home nursing a thumb joint swollen to the size of a tennis ball.

To non-swimmers, a sore thumb may sound something of a trifle, but such an injury can seriously affect a swimmer's speed, especially at the turns. A rushed trip for an X ray proved, to our relief, that no bones were broken. However, it meant even more days off in order to rest it. Wet packs were applied and healing ointment. Again there was nothing to do but wait.

When Murray had finally caught up his training and was ready to join the rest of the team, he had swum well over two hundred miles in this pool alone.

In spite of the anxieties and difficulties there, whenever I think of that stay in Townsville, my pictures glow with warmth. I see again, from our balcony, the dark silhouettes of palm trees against a sunset-reddened sea. I glimpse the strangely fragile, pale green lizards who slept every night on our kitchen ceiling. I walk through the little tropical park and cover the goods in my basket with the pristine whiteness of frangipani flowers. Most of all I remember the spirit of that wonderful team and their determined hard work so cheerfully done.

Thank you, Townsville, for all of these things. Little did we know that the whole scene would be re-enacted when we visited you again before the Olympics in Rome.

On arriving in Brisbane we found that it still lived up to our previous holiday memories. It was the same city of flowers and friendliness. The same atmosphere of brightness pervaded everywhere. It had been here that sports writers had first labeled Murray "the Golden Boy of Swimming." And here again, he was to prove that he and luck were still on the best of terms.

As I ate breakfast out among the roses of our temporary Brisbane home, the lazy drone of insects worked their therapeutic charm on tensed-up nerves. I began to see this time as an unexpected detour away from the strain and pressure of the highway—a detour that was beautifully and quietly refreshing, bringing a welcome respite and uplift.

The boys had borrowed a car to take them along the rough country roads to and from the pool. It could only be called a mobile miracle. I could hear the labored chugging long before the athletes appeared at the gate. "It seems to have no brakes, no gear box, and only half a motor," they explained, laughing at my anxiety. "But somehow it keeps on going." And so did the work of the team in the windup of its training program. The many hours of work and miles of swimming now began to pay off.

Murray found the best medicine to full recovery was a world-record swim over the 400-meter long course distance.

With hope and belief fully restored, he set off with the rest of the team on the last stage of their Olympic journey.

## CHAPTER 13

## MORE TRIALS

On our way to Melbourne, the Olympic city, we stopped off in Sydney for a few days at home, and then away on the next exciting hop. For our team it would mean further hard work and final trials before the Olympic representatives would be chosen.

As we flew the six hundred miles of the final lap, I gave a last look at these bronzed and glorious youngsters, each hoping for the honor of representing his country. Had ever a plane carried a more valuable cargo? Never a more inspiring one, I felt very sure.

Ian had covered the distance by car, taking everything we might possibly need—blankets, linen, electrical equipment, and a store of hard-to-get foods. Australia has some of the finest airlines in the world, which is perhaps why its roads are numbered among the worst. On that trip between Sydney and Melbourne he found the main roads impassable because of floods. Although he was determined to be at the airport to meet us, Ian's schedule had left no margin for such hazards. There was no alternative but to retrace his way and drive across rain-sodden fields to reach the back routes, then to drive at a furious pace to make up for lost time.

Service stations are not over frequent in that part of the country, and on one stretch he limped up to the first gas pump in miles, and discovered that his car's oil sump was totally and completely empty. "By rights you should have been stuck out in the bush somewhere!" he was informed by a puzzled mechanic.

Later he told me of roadsides dotted with wild flowers and narrow lanes made cathedral-like with springtime foliage, but he had passed with no mind or time to enjoy them, then. All that I knew when alighting from the plane was that Ian was there with his unlimited blessings of advice, help, and companionship. Little did I realize as I saw him waiting how greatly I was going to need those things. Why so much had to happen in so short a time was beyond our calculations and needed a student of philosophy to explain. It was certainly a period of the greatest tests— but even greater rewards.

Happy and wonderfully fit again, Murray left with the team on our first afternoon for a tryout in the new and spectacular swimming pool, housed in an ultra-modern stadium which had yet to know the tumult of excited crowds or the splash of a racing dive. It was, in fact, so freshly built that the starting blocks were still unsanded and dangerously slippery to an unwary swimmer. On taking his first header into the pool, Murray crashed down on the sharp concrete edge, tearing a deep gash from ankle to knee.

They brought him back home white, sick, and half fainting. For a second I thought my heart would break for him. So near to his goal and now maybe far away.

This was no way to think.

There was only *one* strength now and I drew on that for calmness and help and belief, knowing it to be a powerful force in helping a quick healing.

For two days and nights we stayed on the job, stanching the bleeding, changing the dressings, trying to make Murray relax and sleep. Naturally, the strain was intense. The shock and anxiety brought on nervous diarrhea and unbearable pains—so bad that all through one night, he rolled on the floor. Even a 4 A.M. game of chess could do little to ease the tension—the pain was too intense to forget. Nor did the newspapers help:

"Our trump card for the Olympic 400 metre event will almost certainly be Sydney's blond vegetarian Murray Rose," said a sports correspondent, "a quietly spoken six footer with one of those copybook strokes that makes record-breaking appear easy."

At a time like this, there is only prayer. Sam, too, was asking for help, I know.

It happened that we knew of a doctor here in Melbourne who believed only in using natural methods—one imbued with the gift of healing in addition to having wise and experienced knowledge. As soon as we were able to get Murray to him, he and his staff made themselves available at any time and for any period. They really performed miracles and so very quickly. Under their healing lamps and special treatments, the gaping wound began to knit together. A few days more and the intestinal trouble and the pains were also relieved. Most of all, they gave Murray back his hope.

Members of the Australian Swimming Union had already announced that, because of his accident, Murray would not be expected to swim in the Trials but would be selected as a member of the Australian Olympic Team on the record of his past great performances. He and his coach had different ideas. "Sam and I have decided to give it a go if I can possibly work it," he told us.

They knew it was essential for Murray to try himself out, to run over the course in the new stadium, and to have personal experience of the vast crowds and tense Olympic atmosphere, and so be prepared for the ordeal of the Games themselves. Drawn and haggard from the great strain of

the past few days, with a fierce red scar down the front
of his leg—he was there, on the starting blocks.

The events of those few days can perhaps best be sum-
marized in the headlines of the press:

October 23: MURRAY ROSE INJURED
October 24: ROSE WITHDRAWS FROM OLYMPIC
SWIMMING TRIALS
" " (later) ROSE MAY SWIM IN 400 RACE
October 25: ROSE'S SHOCK SWIM PLANS—READY FOR
TONIGHT'S RELAY RACE
October 27: CRASH! ROSE WRECKS WORLD TIME: GREAT SWIM!
October 31: ROSE OLYMPIC FAVORITE AFTER SECOND WORLD
RECORD

Of these, the night of the trial for the 1500-meter event
was the most important, by far, in Murray's young life.

Ian, for long a student of planetary influences, had
always forecast for Murray "tremendous success in the
Melbourne Olympics after much trial and difficulty."
Whether the stars had anything to do with it or whether
the predictions had just built up confidence, Murray made
the most of it by establishing two world records, and in-
cidentally becoming the first man in the world to swim
1500 meters in less than eighteen minutes.

Next morning sports writers all through the world hailed
this swim as the equivalent of the first breaking of the
four-minute mile in the field of athletics. Of course, the
barrier has been crossed many times since, and Murray's
best time for this distance is now close to 17 minutes.

In describing the Olympic trials to his swimming readers
in England, Carl Wootton, with whom Murray had
trained when visiting that country, four years earlier,
wrote:

Murray Rose stood out, head and shoulders as the greatest
of all swimmers. A week before the trials he was laid low

with a severe stomach upset and then, returning to training, slipped on a starting block, cutting his leg badly and bruising his shoulder . . . On the Saturday, still under the effects of his accident, he swam the 400 metres and, in spite of missing his fifth turn, scored a brilliant 4:27, the fastest time ever recorded in the world on a long course . . . The 1500 metres on Tuesday had been eagerly awaited as another triumph for Murray Rose. Then, only hours before the event, came drama with the news that George Breen who, in the USA in June had knocked down Furuhashi's six-year-old 1500 metres record to 18:05.9, had now slashed Ford Konno's 800 metres world record by no less than 15s. From this it appeared that to level Breen's performance Murray would have to become the first man in the world to beat 18 minutes for the distance. In face of his recent injuries could he be expected to do it? That was the question.

Murray set off confidently and it was obvious that he had thrown off the effects of his injuries. 100 metres, 1:06.6; 200 metres, 2:18.3; 400 metres, 4:41.9; 750 metres, 8:56. Now it looked as though he might not reach the target but his rhythm did not falter his pace increased, till, to a roar from the crowd, he flashed down the last 50 metres in 34.3s. So, with a time of 17:59.5 Murray Rose became the first swimmer in the world to swim 1500 metres in under 18 minutes.

A tall, plump Japanese was the first to congratulate Murray as he climbed out of the water. He was Hironoshin Furuhashi, who held the world 1500-meter record of 18 min 19 secs for six years until Breen had broken it a few months before.

"Murray must win the Olympic gold medal," Furuhashi said. "The others haven't the potential of this one."

Over the closing laps of the race it had been obvious that Murray was likely to break Breen's world mark—and the capacity crowd cheered every stroke.

As he turned for the last stretch—more than 50 meters ahead of his nearest opponent, the applause was deafening.

Then the pool announcer said that Murray couldn't miss and the uproar became even louder.

When it was all over, Murray stood waiting on his starting block, with a yellow towel round his neck contrasting with his green "lucky" swim shorts. The announcer began to read his time as "seventeen minutes . . ." And the crowd went wild.

He was the first human to break eighteen minutes for this distance. It was more than ten seconds before the announcer could make himself heard to tell the remainder of the time. After the race Murray told how the crowd had helped him.

He told the press: "It is very satisfying to know the crowd is on your side when you are swimming for a record.

"The time surprised me.

"I heard the crowd whistling and yelling and thought I was swimming well. But I felt I was behind schedule early in the race and kept my fingers crossed while waiting to hear the time."

He added:

"When I saw what Breen had done to my old world record, I wanted to make it all square. But I believe Breen will be going after my new time in a couple of days. I may not hold it very long."

Murray reaffirmed that his main object in the Olympics would be his "pet distance"—400 meters.

Meanwhile the Australian press was commenting: "Sydney's 'blond torpedo,' Murray Rose, smashed the world's long pool record and proved himself without doubt the best middle distance swimmer in the world when he won the 400 metres freestyle." Murray himself said: "Frankly, it could have been better. I felt much too fresh when I'd finished. I hope to improve on that in the Games." Whatever his future wishes, the first rim of Olympic success had appeared in the sky.

Between the trials and the opening of the games, the strain was slackened off a little. We found time to look around and absorb more of the meaning of this Great Athletic Get-Together.

It is a warm, colorful, and moving experience to be part of an Olympic Village—or even close to it . . . to see every day the special Olympic buses drive through the Village gates with chosen athletes, newly arrived from some far distant country . . . to watch that country's standard being proudly unfurled till finally, as nation after nation takes up residence, the entrance drive is flanked by two waving lines of color.

Some six thousand athletes and officials were to make this settlement their home for two or three weeks. To see the world thus, in microcosm, away from politics and brought together through shared goals, was something we might do well to remember.

We had long since made the heart-warming discovery that barriers go down easily in this camaraderie of sport. Those invisible curtains, which all too often cut off freedom and understanding between peoples, are effortlessly drawn aside. Class distinction melts away and tightly closed doors are thrown open in welcome to one who has been tried and proven through sport.

Race, creed, and custom are quite naturally put in their superficial places; warm friendships are formed and hospitality extended between those living in countries apart. Perhaps most significant of all, the unsure and over-sensitive individual will find new heart and encouragement. Isn't there an inspiring formula here that we, living in our hidebound world of conformities, might follow?

These thoughts take over as one walks through such a Village. The youngsters we saw there were obviously influenced by them too. A brown-eyed, short-plaited gymnast from Milan sat sipping a milk shake with a gangling Russian runner as they watched an Australian act on television. Neither could understand a word, yet both were happy as on a picnic.

An American group outside their brand-new cottages started an impromptu square dance and called a "Hi there!" to a couple of passing Rumanians. The Rumanians couldn't understand either, but all were caught up in the friendliness which ran like a thread of warm color through the world's newest city.

Many of the groups were happy just to sing, to listen to radiograms, to exchange their pesos, drachmas, lire, and dollars for stuffed koala bears, toy kangaroos, or boomerangs carrying the five Olympic rings and a miscellany of souvenirs in the stores that were doing brisk business at the entrance to the village. "If the United Nations could get on a basis like this, things could be different," said the Village Commandant, "and yet these people are meeting on an intensively competitive as well as a common ground."

For Murray and the other swimmers the fifty meters of water in Melbourne's new Olympic pool had become the most important stretch of water in the world. And not only to swimmers. Intending spectators had bought out all seats for every final event a year before the stadium was finished. So great was the enthusiasm for swimming that the pool was opened to the public daily and lines 600 yards long waited several hours for admission just to watch training sessions. Over 20,000 people a day paid to see the teams just in *training*.

This was Murray's headquarters for three weeks. It was the meeting place of old-time swimmers from the Games of the past, from Helsinki, London, and Berlin. It was the rendezvous of famous coaches and sporting personalities from all over the world who once every four years, in the year of the Olympiad, are drawn like homing pigeons to this small rectangle of water in whichever country, however distant, it may be. There were many new faces on the international scene that will long be remembered—Yamanaka, for instance, the powerful Japanese who gave Murray such a struggle in both the 400- and 1500-meter events. As the two boys, representative of two vastly different countries and cultures exchanged badges and photographs, my mind went back thirteen years to when Australia was at war with a million Yamanakas.

It was as though my half-formed thought had formed words in another's mind, because a few days later the following letter appeared in an Australian paper:

Sir,—The happy, inspiring picture in the "Herald" of Australia's Murray Rose and Japan's Tsuyoshi Yamanaka in an Olympic embrace should be the answer to those who criticize the value of the Olympic Games. Ten years ago such a photograph would have been considered impossible. Pearl Harbor ushered in an era of hatred against the Japanese, a hatred which is slow to disappear. We Australians cannot forget the grim horrors of those war years, but we are gradually forgiving the Japanese. The arrival of Japanese brides, the increasing Australian-Japanese trade relations and the Olympic welcome to these innocent Japanese youngsters all are auguries of a peaceful and prosperous future of the Pacific for both countries.

This sort of thing, repeated so many times during these Olympic weeks, is the true essence of the Games.

The Russians? I think they were very much the same as all the others, though it would have been hard to reach their hearts, so closely were they guarded by those in charge. The Russian officials recognized that they had a lot to learn about swimming. They timed, watched, filmed, and made notes on nearly every swimmer in the pool. It wasn't until the last day of the Games that they approached the Aussie coaches to ask their "secrets," believing that it would be unfair to ask for such knowledge to be shared before the last race was swum.

As the eight fierce days of heats and finals drew near we found that our hardest times were by no means behind us. Murray lived and slept at the Village and had to drive the three miles to our home for all his meals since the commissary was not prepared to handle a specialized non-meat menu. At first, this journey had been fairly easy until schedules became more difficult to keep. Competitors had to follow a split-second regime. Crowds became thicker and more difficult to push through. The mass of autograph seekers at the Village gates became more demanding and a prospective Olympic champion, alone, and on foot was easy game.

We asked, we pleaded with the team manager for some relaxation of the rules, to allow time for the bare essentials of proper meals and rest; he passed on our request to the sectional manager and thence to officials of the Australian Olympic Body. At such times the official mind appears to move relentlessly along machinelike lines. There can be no appealing to an "official heart."

At last the answer came in a firm direction from a doctor who summed up the critical situation and who had the authoritative backing of a medical degree. With precious little time before the start of the Games, the rigidity of red tape was somewhat relaxed, thus enabling Murray to get a full quota of meals and the benefits of his usual pre-race program.

The day of the Opening Ceremony was a miracle in itself. After cold, dull weather which had chilled the bones of visitors from such places as Fiji or Trinidad, this historic day, which inaugurated the first Olympics to be held outside the Northern Hemisphere, blazed forth, brilliant and shining. It was as though the gods all smiled at once, and there was every reason why they should, for these gods of ancient

Greece, Norway, India, and the Orient—were merged into one, a deeply felt and inspiring Presence.

Many are drawn by the color of this stirring spectacle, and yet, as it passes, it is not so much the sight as the spirit which moves them most—doubly impressive by its age-old symbolism. The runner with the flame still alight from ages past, and staying alight for Olympians yet to come . . . the cloud of encircling pigeons with their message of peace . . . the time-honored Olympic banner slowly raised once again . . . the uplifting hymn and the proud marching of vibrant youth . . . color after color . . . standard after standard. Wearing hats, caps, berets, and turbans—every athlete takes the salute as he passes the official dais.

When I saw Murray going by, I hoped that something of the message of this day would stay with him always. I am sure that it will. Everyone present was no doubt thinking the same sort of thing. If only we could all hang on to this Unity of Spirit!

There were few who did not show the gleam of a tear at some time during that ceremony. Only a pretty hardened soul could have remained unmoved.

Our last obstacle came the day before the first Olympic swimming race. It was one common to all athletes on such occasions, a case of just plain jitters. During the last workout, Murray became apprehensive about his form. Had he lost his rhythm? Was his stroking as co-ordinated as it should be? Waiting for weeks in first-class shape, trying to hold on to top condition—this period had all the swimmers nervously on edge.

Up to now, Murray had managed to fulfill the belief of those around him—but this was a responsibility bigger by far than any he had yet been called upon to face. Still only seventeen, he had by no means reached full muscular development. He was up against the finest champions in the world. His success would add to the prestige and honor of his country. In addition to all that, he must uphold the great humanitarian ideals he had been brought up to represent—no wonder the load suddenly felt heavy.

Since there was no real reason for any loss of confidence, it was necessary to remove the subconscious doubt. Such fears are usually quite forgotten the moment a swimmer hits the water. But when the stakes are high, everything possible must be done to eliminate chance. Quite fortuitously we had met a qualified psychologist, who had once been a swimmer himself. He at once grasped the situation and in one helpful talk removed all unnecessary tensions.

The first of several great days appeared on the horizon—one that had been dimly reflected twelve years before. Murray awoke feeling fine, ready to give of his very best. That was all there was to it.

## CHAPTER 14

## REACHING FOR THE GOAL

"The final of the Men's World Freestyle 200-meter relay," came the voice of the announcer, "Lane 1, Germany; Lane 2, Australia . . ." Australia's four fastest freestylers moved up to the starting blocks, Murray among them. My mind telescoped into a fraction of a second the long preparation, the trials and triumphs that all of these boys had known—just for this moment. Merely to swim as *one leg* of the relay team any one of the squad would have given all he had.

Japan, the United States, and Australia had all swum several substitutes in competing the "heats." Now the fresh, rested, shock troops moved in for Australia to win the event in world-record time and mark the start of a big comeback in a sport which, for some years, had been dominated by other nations.

"Once you get in the water with them you just can't catch them," said American team captain, Ford Konno.

It was Murray's first gold medal.

Next day he faced his first individual race—the final of the 400 meters.

From an entry of thirty-eight swimmers in five "heats," Murray had already qualified with the fastest time and was given the center lane for the final. "Break 4:34 and make sure of the key middle lane in the final," Sam had told him. Murray made sure with a 4:31.7.

Tense though I was during the final of that race, I have a

clear picture of it and found time to enjoy watching the different styles. The American, George Breen, plowing and crashing a course through the water . . . Yamanaka with a lopsided pull that made his body bounce up and down in a clockwork rhythm that once having been set in motion seemed never likely to stop or even slow down. Then Murray with his longer, smoother strokes . . . relaxed, fluent, sure.

"He's doing fine," Ian whispered. "No need to worry."

How grateful I always am for his understanding presence at these peak moments of tension!

This is how the Melbourne *Age* described the race next morning:

Last night's success was the culmination of a 12 year preparation of Rose by Herford. To show their complete understanding, I repeat what happened before the race last night. Herford went to see Rose and asked how he felt. Rose replied: "I feel terrible. My legs are all shaky." Herford responded: "I feel the same way and when we both feel like that you usually do something good." That is a mild description of what Rose did some 15 minutes later.

The tall 17-year-old from Sydney swam with amazing confidence, content to lie second or third for the first 200 metres. American, George Breen, led for the first 100 metres in 62.6 secs., his rough stroking contrasting sharply with the smooth, easy-flowing style of the Australian. Then the 17-year-old Japanese, Yamanaka took over, with Rose second. Breen spurted to match Rose, but it was obviously an effort taking great strain of his resources. Rose edged up to touch with Yamanaka at the 200 metre mark in 2.11.6 and then crept ahead a half-yard in the next lap. It was intelligent, confident swimming. Rose had the longer-stroking, Yamanaka stretching to match him. Whilst Breen's ruggedness became even more untidy as he strove to hold his ground.

The relentless pacing of Rose, with laps of 34.8 secs. and

34 secs., made the others crack by the 300 metre mark, Yamanaka dropping a yard behind, with a yard and a half to Breen. Rose seemed to be swimming quite leisurely, with scarcely a splash as his arms neatly threaded through the water. Yamanaka began to "belt" the water and lost "form." A 34.2 sec. last lap left Rose a clear leader as he turned for home, but he decided to make sure of it and sprinted away with a 32.7 effort to score a 5 yard triumph. Rose's final time of 4.27.3 was only .6 outside the world record, set in a short-course pool. Murray Rose will appear again, in the first heat of the 1500 metre freestyle, and he should qualify effortlessly. Herford claimed Rose was still not at his peak but had proved himself the greatest all-round swimmer the world had seen.

I don't think I ever doubted that Murray would take this race, but the nervous strain is always intense, and I remember Sam's wonderful wife, Thora, throwing her arms around me in sheer relief as together we watched Murray step up and receive his second gold medal from Prince Axel of Denmark.

The national anthem was played, and the standard of Australia slowly raised—this time for Murray. Applause and cheering broke out again. "You beaut!" "Good on yer, mate!"

The movie men, TV cameras, and reporters from papers across the world moved in, and it was late before our Olympic champion could get to sleep and start preparing for the most grueling test of the Games.

"I am hoping that Rose will win the 1500 meters to become the youngest person ever to record this unusual feat," said Sam. "In the 1500 meters he will not go out to break the world record, just to win his race. But if they push him, he will break the record."

We did not have long to wait for this, the last event of the Games. Nor did Murray have long to rest. As the champions went to the starting blocks for the heats on the following afternoon, Murray seemed to be the competitor most favored to win. The world record for this distance was his, barely a month old. George Breen was said to be capable of beating this.

Murray was not drawn against Breen in the "heat," but instead had to meet the Japanese, Yamanaka. Main interest in the first heat centered on the duel between these two boys. In the first of the thirty laps of the pool, the Jap took a small lead which he had increased to one yard at the 100-meters mark and to three yards after 400 meters.

"What is Rose doing?" the crowd was beginning to ask. "Is he racing or just swimming in order to qualify for the finals?"

Despite an athlete's well-laid plans, the tactics of an adversary can upset them completely. Even a heat is a race to a sports-loving crowd, and tension rose as Yamanaka increased his lead to four yards at 800 meters. Then the change set in and inch by inch, lap after lap, Murray crept up on the fighting Japanese, till with only two laps to go he had reduced the lead to only a foot. Then Murray put on the pressure, going to a clear lead. Yamanaka responded and down the last lap nearly caught Murray to touch the wall only a tenth of a second behind.

It was the third heat for that race that provided the real fireworks when George Breen, instead of being content merely to qualify, shocked the swimming world by turning in a dazzling 17 min 52.9 secs, reducing Murray's world record, established in this same pool, a few weeks earlier, by a clear 6.6 seconds.

There was a lot of open questioning next day as to whether it had been the best thing for Breen to turn in so fast a time in a preliminary heat. The Australian coaches said frankly that it was most unwise of George to make a maximum effort at a time when it didn't really matter. To

Sam and Murray it was worth a great deal in a prior assessment of an opponent's capabilities.

"He should have saved that one for Friday night," said Sam. "It will take too much out of him." But Breen who thrives on hard work, was emphatic that he had not put too much effort into the swim. "I felt good so I opened up over the second half," he said after the race.

Asked whether he could repeat his record-breaking performance in the finals, Breen said: "I don't know. I guess so. That's the one I have to win. I just swam tonight. There was no tension. I had no worries. I felt good so I swam well. I won't know till tomorrow if it took anything out of me."

Until Breen had broken the record, Murray was a 3 to 1 favorite. Now Murray dropped to an even-money bet. Plenty of money was placed on both competitors, as the race promised to be one of the greatest thrillers of the Olympics.

"The best single event of the 1956 Olympics and some of the best swimming in history is expected tomorrow night," the New York *Times* promised its readers. "Competing on opposite sides of the world hitherto, Rose and Breen have had to swim only against the clock. Other entrants were always left far up the pool. But tomorrow night they will be together in the same race."

Their correspondent in Australia continued: "Breen is a phenomenon. He swims as if he were a rank amateur. He flails at the water like a lop-sided windmill. His kick is so feeble it serves to do little more than stabilize him.

"In contrast the smooth-stroking Rose is one of the most elegant swimming stylists in the world. It would seem that Breen wouldn't have a chance when the two swim side by side. But Breen's times speak for themselves. And his competitive determination will make him a hard man to beat, provided he didn't leave his best swim in the pool in his record-breaking heat."

Some Australian experts favored Murray, some favored Breen. All of them commented that Murray was going into what was to be the greatest test of his career without any specialized preparation for the distance event. Breen was essentially a distance swimmer. The fact that Murray beat him comfortably over the 400 distance was no indication that he would do so in the marathon.

All Murray's training for the past three years had been with one objective in mind—a gold medal in the 400-meters freestyle, which he had already won. The swimmers had one full day to prepare themselves for the battle ahead. What does an Olympic athlete do during those periods of waiting?

He plays cards and dominoes in the Village, makes friends with athletes from round the world, watches television, listens to the music of guitars and accordions, gets lost in folk songs from faraway lands, and tries to forget what the newspapers outside are saying about him.

But forgetfulness of Murray's impending race was impossible. Everywhere people were speculating on the outcome. Somehow, for a few brief days, it had caught and held the imagination of Melbourne—embracing the world of shops, elevators, buses, and taxis. This was more than a race; national pride and sentiment were tied up with it too. There was one person whose belief never faltered—our dear Sam. I can imagine how much courage and faith he passed on to Murray during those apprehensive days.

To the press, Sam said: "I am confident Murray will come through with flying colors. He will win. Nobody has yet seen Rose at his best. They'll see it in the final of the 1500. Whatever Breen can do, Rose can do better. I'll stake my reputation on it."

## CHAPTER 15

## MURRAY'S GOLDEN FINISH

We awoke early that December morning, and immediately our minds tensed with apprehension as we remembered the marathon struggle which lay ahead of Murray. The sun was warm from the start and pointing its bright fingers through the cracks of our blinds. My own first thought was one of great thankfulness at having Ian here with us again, at last. His quiet strength and deep insight smoothed out many a worry before it began. His tender humor could turn pent-up moments into ones of laughter. He could always be relied upon to unearth our off-beat foods in the most unlikely places; to organize schedules; deal promptly with unforeseen difficulties and any official problems which, since we lived to a different set of rules, were a constant factor. His presence wonderfully lifted the load, and helped to give our air-castles a solid, practical foundation.

Before any crisis or challenging event, one's emotions seem to be wired to some high-tension battery, and the slightest reminder sparks an electric shock. At such a time the most trivial incidents make an impression for life. This *was* such a day! But in describing this, we might just as well be taking the reader through our experiences on any one of the hundreds of big championship days, both before and after this one.

Moving quietly, so that Murray might stock up on every second's worth of sleep, I put on a robe and crept out into the little fenced-in garden. Instinctively I sought its early morning serenity as a shield against the pressures of the next few hours.

It was utterly quiet—and yet not still—for one sensed the powerful industry of nature, the unquestioning inevitability of each tiny life, rhythmically working towards perfection. I tried to attune the mind to the Source which guides such things—and be guided by it too.

An Olympic race may be of minute importance in terms of eternity, but it completely absorbed us at this moment, and its challenge was a very big reality. I thought of the other competing champions, who would also be calling upon any extra help they could find, each having an equal right and the same opportunity of reaching his greatest strength and giving his finest performance. Surely, we cannot ask for any *special* favors, for the same power is intrinsic within us all. Pleading for the gratification of personal desire could never be the way of achievement. What, then, can we do? We can open ourselves to the flow of cosmic energy. We can ask to be kept aware of the Infinite Power of God, and we can tune in to it and draw upon it. As we give way to doubts and fears, our ability to work harmoniously and fully with this "built-in powerhouse," will be that much lessened. If we can accept the knowledge that we are, at all times, a dedicated instrument being guided and helped in our achievements, then we shall find ourselves expressing more of His desires, and His strength.

Trying to hang on to these "whisperings," I walked back to the house. A neighbor's kitten was clawing at the bright yellow "AUSTRALIA" emblazoned on an Olympic towel. I lifted it into my arms and carried its carefree sweetness to share with the others.

As I began to set breakfast out on the patio I could hear laughter and the usual scuffle for first in the bathroom. I knew that sudden warmth, which creeps over us senti-

mental ones at just being a part of a family—the sort of
family which wholly justifies our purpose for being here at
all.

Still joking, Ian and Murray sat down to breakfast. Then
Sam arrived, bringing with him his usual ability to recharge our confidence and enthusiasm. Murray was obviously relieved to see him, and they went off together to dis-
cuss the tactics of the race, and to plan the strategy, lap by
lap.

"The kid's in great form," Sam assured us, as we watched
Murray climb into his little, battered, borrowed car and
take off for the Village, his usual quiet smile denying the
tense anxiety. "We all know it's going to be tough, but he's
swimming in great form, and has the mental attitude to win.
I have no doubts—no doubts whatever. And you two better
have none either."

Then, giving me a reassuring hug, he left with instructions to "give the boy the full works and have him on the
blocks in peak condition."

Ian went out, too, and, having no time to spare at beauty
parlors, I started to shampoo my hair. The doorbell rang.
Wrapped only in a towel, and dripping with suds, I called
to ask who was there. "It's a reporter from *Sports Illustrated*," came the reply, "I was told that Murray Rose was
here."

As we had kept our whereabouts dark, I thought I was
safe from such news seekers. I called back that Murray was
not there—neither was Mr. Rose, and I was taking a bath,
and my hair was soaking wet. "Never mind," the voice persisted, "put on some clothes, and tie up your hair. I will
wait in the cab." And he did wait too. The American journalist was both friendly and disarming and made it quite
impossible to remain ruffled for long. For an hour or more
he fired questions, while the taxi meter ticked away outside.

I went back to my hairdressing—only to have another

caller—but this was a very different kind of visitor. A gentle-faced stranger with an armful of flowers, she explained that she had brought them with thoughts of good luck from several of the neighbors. Until that moment I had felt an outsider, but this loving gesture gave a sense of belonging, after all.

One tried, of course, to keep one's mind on anything other than the race, but this was utterly impossible. When I went to the local drugstore for a fresh supply of massage oil, the assistant and his customer were discussing the outcome of tonight's big swim, each giving reasons for the favorite they were backing. Not only did the daily newspapers carry front page headlines about "Tonight's Great Race," but newsboys carried placards announcing the coming fight between Breen, Yamanaka, and Rose. On returning home, Ian had many similar stories to tell. The conversation in the barber's shop had become quite heated as bets were exchanged on each champion. Even the elevator attendant in a public building was laying the odds and preparing for a long wait outside the swimming stadium later that night.

We were by no means alone with our jitters. Reports from the Village grapevine showed that the other contestants were extremely tense and edgy. While Murray gave us the news of the morning he ate a large bunch of muscatels, knowing their glucose content to be easily assimilated and turned into extra strength. Murray's main meal of the day was planned for five hours prior to the swim. If too much food is taken too close to a race, the digestive process will not be completed, nor a full store of energy be available.

When even a split second might change the outcome of a race, nothing is too trivial to be overlooked. Murray took his razor out into the garden and proceeded to smooth away all the hair from his legs. "It may be a mere psychological factor," he explained, "but it does give a clean, sharp feeling when moving through the water and it prevents a 'hair breadth' of drag when a critical burst of speed is vital." We talked of inconsequential nothings in the way one always does when avoiding a tense subject.

The arrival of the mailman with a stack of telegrams and letters brought a further much-needed digression. We found warmly helpful messages from friends we knew—and many, many more from those we'd never met. They would have been glad to know how close they seemed on that pent-up afternoon. Each sincere wish and moving prayer added its share of courage and determination and frequently brought tears of gratitude.

We are often asked what a non-meat-eating champion eats on such an occasion. This was a simple enough salad meal including lettuce, grated carrots, peas, and four or five egg yolks barely warmed in tomato juice, then slices of millet toast, and a small portion of cooked millet to which was added sesame meal, dates, and honey.

No sooner had Murray finished his meal and gone to sleep than a group of small children chose a spot right under his window for a screaming game of cops and robbers. However, a few words and a two-shilling piece sent them off to the drugstore for ice cream sodas. All was very, very quiet.

While Ian was answering some of Murray's fan mail, I picked up a favorite book of quieting thoughts to still those tummy "butterflies." I ironed my very old but "lucky" blue dress and for extra good fortune took out a certain gold brooch in the form of a Union Jack. This had been a gift from Sir Frank Beaurepaire, the man mainly responsible for our being in this place, for his dream had come true when the Olympic Games were awarded to Melbourne. He, too, once represented his country as a swimmer and had worked tirelessly to bring the Olympics to his city, a city that had made him Lord Mayor for this great year. Tragically, a few weeks previously, while in a barber's chair, he had suddenly died. I was thinking of this unquenchable, exuberant little man and the poignant ending of his dream. The sun was setting, and the rich notes of a blackbird was the only sound I could hear.

"I'm afraid it's time to wake Murray." Ian's voice jumped me back to earth. Murray was still sound asleep and far removed from the coming contest. For a moment I almost wished that the Greeks had never thought up the idea of the Olympic Games. Almost with regret I began the usual half-hour massage in order to stimulate the muscles to give of their best and to lessen fatigue and pain during the long, hard race. This left barely enough time for a shower and a spoonful or two of Irish moss jelly, some tahini, and honey.

"Okay, Murray, it's time we get going," Ian called from the car.

Wearing the green and yellow sweat suit of the Australian team, Murray climbed in beside his father. Neighbors stood outside and called out wishes of hope and good luck. As we started off on the eight-mile journey to the Games arena, we heard the soft spraying of water sprinklers and could smell the perfume of roses and night-scented stocks. I almost envied those neighbors the quiet routine of their evening as they settled down to a family supper and tuned in to a favorite sportscaster. And yet, had I been challenged, I would not have changed places with anyone in the world.

Every car for miles around Melbourne seemed to be converging onto the same spot. As we crawled past row after row of identical red-bricked urban villas we were constantly blocked by traffic jams. Murray was very quiet and became increasingly apprehensive as the time for the start of the race grew closer. I leaned forward and tried to relax the tenseness by massaging the nerve centers between his shoulders. None of us, in fact, could think of much to say until we came in sight of the glittering decorations surrounding the Olympic center. As we approached the colorful modern structure which housed the pool, the density of the crowd forced us to a standstill. Hundreds were waiting around the gateway in the hope of obtaining canceled tickets or to catch a glimpse of the competing champions.

Ian turned to Murray: "Well, here we are. Good luck, boy. You'll be all right, I know."

Murray climbed out looking almost deathly white, and I handed him his bag of towels and swim trunks. One's whole being longs to help, to lift some of the strain, to say the right words. But there's nothing one can do but lovingly kiss a blessing and watch an outwardly relaxed young man smiling and waving as he pushes through the cheering crowd. The last I could see of Murray was the gay little tassel swinging from the top of his cap as it disappeared into the competitors' entrance.

But above the gate one exceptionally bright star seemed nearer than all the others. I'm sure many white hairs and a shortened life span must have resulted from that hour or so of waiting for the starter's gun.

As we took our place in the swarm of bodies and inched our way towards the jammed turnstiles we heard people offering double and treble the price to anyone willing to relinquish his ticket. We saw other enthusiasts who had climbed the high fence and were standing on the sills of the windows while others patiently gathered outside and prepared to wait for news of the race.

Among these was an old friend of the family who, having failed to obtain a seat, felt impelled to stay close to hear how things were going. The mother of three boys herself, she was trembling with nerves on Murray's behalf.

"I feel quite ill," she said as we passed, "poor Murray, I can hardly stand the strain!" Such emotions did little to bolster our thoughts. I remember answering: "I will not listen to a single doubt. Murray *will* win. Have no fear on that score!"

Many of Murray's school friends were among the crowd. They also expressed their jitters and brought little help.

Then we heard the cheerful greeting of John Marshall, that great and well-loved champion of three Olympics, known and admired also in America during his years at Yale. John had been Murray's inspiration from the start of his swimming career. (Tragically, a car accident took his life soon after these Games.)

"I'm just on my way to cheer your son on to victory but first I'll have a word with him in the dressing room. No one knows that pre-race feeling better than I do. I'll try to kid him out of it!" We never saw John again.

We found our places on the hard wooden seats as we had so many times before and smelled the warm dampness which, for us, had become synonymous with suppressed excitement.

The competitors were having their pre-race warmup while coaches looked on anxiously. One by one they disappeared into the dressing room. The crowd was dense. Even the aisle ways were blocked with spectators. The Duke of Edinburgh, Prime Minister Menzies, and other notables had taken their places just in front of us. The Duke, a few days previously, had asked to have Murray introduced to him. Unfortunately, the swimming officials had had to explain that Murray was preparing for a maximum effort which didn't end until the last day—in fact the very last race—of the Games. However, in Sydney recently, Murray more than made up for that disappointment when he was privileged to board the royal yacht, *Britannia,* and have luncheon with both Her Majesty the Queen and the Duke.

As I sat looking at the now empty and glassily still pool I pictured the thousands who would be tuned into this spot at this moment. There would be families on lonely outback farms, wealthy diners in famous clubs. At Murray's school in Sydney, we were told later, a dance was in progress, but not one person danced until the race was over.

The crowd was silent and tense as the boys came slowly out, wearing the sweat suits of their country . . . Japan, the United States, Canada, France. The eight fastest swimmers in the world over the 1500-meter distance were all together at this moment. No fewer than three of them were Australians. All three had swum against each other every Saturday morning from Murray's very first days at the Bondi Club. Now they were here, fighting it out with him still.

This is the moment they had trained for month after month—hour upon weary hour. And that *look* was there in the champions' eyes—a veiled look, a turning inward in an effort to master tension and overcome doubt and fear. In the outward false nonchalance one senses the forced stilling of excited, anxious nerves.

Sweat suits were quietly, slowly removed in an overstatement of relaxation. There were handshakes between the competitors—the starter's command to mount the blocks—and the eyes are clear and alert again.

After the firing of the gun I hardly dared look. I prayed that Murray might be made calm and sure during that great battle, wasting nothing in panic and fear; only that his full strength and courage and ability would be with him all the way through, proving among other things, that stamina and endurance have nothing to do with eating meat. Afterwards, we learned of others who were praying, too, people we had never met and people we had never known until they wrote. "We have watched this shy, fair-headed youngster from a baby, and felt we wanted to be near him, and ask for strength to be given in his greatest test . . ."

Sometimes I covered my eyes and sometimes I looked, as lap after lap was left behind. The large numbers at the end of each lane were changed as a competitor made yet another turn, telling him for how many more laps he must nurse his aching muscles and conserve his diminishing strength.

Twenty-seven laps to go—twenty-five—twenty-three—slowly, slowly those thirty laps of the 50-meter pool were cut down. Murray passed Breen soon after the fifteenth lap.

"Did you feel Breen weaken at that stage?" a reporter asked Murray after the race.

"I wasn't thinking about Breen weakening," Murray laughed. "If he had known how I was feeling he would have won the race by a mile!"

All three swimmers kept close together for the first eight laps with Breen just ahead and Yamanaka lying second. Then the pattern altered, and with only inches separating the three, Yamanaka drew ahead at 800 meters and then, remorselessly, inch by inch, Murray overhauled first Breen, then Yamanaka, with three colossal bursts.

Murray was stroking evenly now, relaxed but apparently full of strength, rhythmic, and fluent to watch.

Breen started to splash, and it became clear that those experts were right who had said: "You can't do two world times in three days." The strain had been too much; he could never make it now.

But the courageous Jap never flagged. Still with that curious clockworklike motion he plugged on and on.

Murray was calling now on that inner reserve that he had stored away, pulling stronger than ever, till at 1400 meters, with only two laps to go, the result seemed settled. Then it was the Jap's turn to make a last fighting effort and pull up nearly three yards on Murray's "blind" side.

"Make him look! Let him see him! Murray! Murray!" screamed those around us as they tried to warn Murray of the danger.

In the last twenty meters Murray realized the desperate challenge and was able to fend it off to touch the wall a body's length ahead.

The deafening roar around the stadium was taken up and continued outside. It leapt quickly along the crowds that lined the river Yarra that night. People jumped and stamped their feet, cheered, and threw programs into the air, while Murray lay back in the water, eyes closed, relaxed at last. Sam leapt the barrier and was down among the competitors, calling, "You little cock-sparrow! You beaut!"

The commentator describing the scene afterwards to the largest radio audience in any sporting event in Australia said: "My heart goes out to this great youngster. I have seen him grow up. I have watched him meet every challenge that was ever put to him. Forgive me for not speaking until I recovered myself after the most magnificent race I have ever watched."

For me, the pool, the packed stadium, the crowd, and those around were hazy and far away. In the distance I could still hear that mighty roar. The biggest cheer of the Games, I was told. One I shall go on hearing for the rest of my life. People kissed me, wrung my hand, threw their arms around me.

It was then that I saw Murray step up for his third gold medal, making him the first boy in the history of the Games to accomplish this feat at the age of seventeen. He shook hands with his two mighty opponents, Yamanaka of Japan and George Breen of America. Then, as one in a trance, he waved—hesitatingly, shyly—in answer to the salutations of the crowd.

One's feelings, at such a moment, are beyond recording—they lift one far above the medium of words.

This was a moment of pure gold and one that I have locked away in my heart. No matter how dreary the days may become, I have a shining treasure there that will always make them bright, and a deep prayer of thankfulness for having found a power beyond my own, where lies a never ending flow of strength and help and love.

There were great rejoicings in the Australian camp that night, for Australia had not only proved a great host to the sporting world but had built a young and strong swimming team such as the world had never seen.

We quickly learned that the whole world loves a champion. Messages came from every part of the globe, and from all kinds of people—great sporting names of the past and the present, congratulations from the heads of the government, from mayors and municipalities, from clubs and societies. Even the home of his ancestors had remembered, for there was a greeting from the Clan Rose in Scotland.

It was thirty-two years since a swimmer had brought off the Olympic hat trick. It was even longer since a man had won the great Olympic swimming double of the metric mile and the quarter mile. No one had ever done either at the youthful age of seventeen.

Quite often I wear a charm bracelet depicting athletic figures, which Murray gave me that day, and the note that came with it, hastily scribbled in pencil, is one that is written in my heart. Next morning, the newspapers singled out as ". . . The heroes of The Games, Vladimir Kuts, Bobby Morrow, and Murray Rose . . ." Ken Knox of the Melbourne *Herald* described Murray as: "The world's best, and most intelligent swimmer." Yet another ran the headlines:

"MIGHTY like a Rose!" An entire front page was devoted to a picture of Murray lying in the water after his big race. They called it "OUR GOLDEN FINISH."

I guess that went for us too.

Eight years have gone by since that "finish" in Melbourne—years continuously colored by athletic goals. Now, suddenly and unexpectedly, swimming pools with their intense anxiety and the applause of cheering crowds no longer fill our world.

In the last few weeks another doll has been added to the collection on my shelf. She is a snow-girl from Canada, and her story is perhaps the most poignantly dramatic of them all, for it tells of the events which so sharply changed Murray's course. Frequently named as a history-making figure, our son was now destined to repeat this role in a less happy light. He became, in fact, the first Olympic champion in good standing, trained and ready to defend his titles, who was denied that right by the very men entrusted with its preservation.

Many readers will remember the incident which caused Murray to be a television commentator, instead of a competitor, at the Tokyo Olympics. The story was the subject of many articles in leading newspapers and magazines throughout the world, never to be forgotten by thousands of dedicated swimmers and officials. One such article is sufficient to recall the sentiments and true events which were recorded by all:

> It must be that the austere Australian Olympic Committee has either forgotten the true meaning of the Olympics, or have sacrificed an honorable athlete on the altar of bureaucratic machination.
>
> We refer to the Olympic champion, Murray Rose.
>
> Rose, who competed in the 1956 and 1960 Olympics for Australia was barred from the XVIII Olympiad because he

had not won his place in the Australian Tryouts in February
(8 months before the Games).

The Australian champion, who has been competing since
he was 7, graduated from the University of So. California
with a degree in telecommunication and acting—a vocation
that permitted him rare opportunities to train and swim.
That he was able to compete is a tribute to his dedication
to the sport. For in pursuing his chosen profession, work
came in the highly irregular manner that is peculiar to his
profession. One such employment opportunity occurred
while the Australians were holding their National Swimming
Championships last February.

Neither the Australian Olympic Federation nor the Amateur Swimming Union of Australia took the time to formally
advise Murray Rose that failure to swim in the Australian
Championships in February would forfeit his chance to compete in the Tokyo games the following October.

With a notable, uncompromising rigidity, Murray Rose
was washed into competitive oblivion, despite the pleas
of Australians from high rank to common citizen.

For Murray is no ordinary athlete. Gus Stager of Michigan
University, and the U.S. Olympic Swim Coach in 1960 said,
"I have to believe that Rose is the greatest swimmer who
ever lived, greater than even Johnny Weissmuller."

And Rose is just that. This summer at Los Altos, after but
a month or so of training, he cracked the listed 1500 meter
world mark with an amazing 17:01.8 clocking. Those who
saw this swim knew he could go faster.

Several weeks later at the Canadian Nationals, in what was
destined to be his last amateur competition, Rose broke
the 880 yd. (lc) world record with an 8:55.5 effort. This
fine swim was of greater significance as it was performed
under extreme conditions. At the time, little did Rose know
that he was through as an amateur . . . for when the incen-
tive of competing in the "supreme" meet of the world is
denied a champion, the will to continue is destroyed forever.

Unlike the U.S. Olympic Committee, who in 1960 offered
a hospitalized Jeff Farrel a place on the U.S. team without

the need to place in a Trial, the Australian authority has allowed blind stubbornness to strike a mature athlete from his dedicated right to compete in the Tokyo Olympics.

For Murray Rose, the flame of the XVIII Olympiad was extinguished before it was ever lit.

By denying Murray a place on their Olympic team, the Australian Swimming Union denied him the chance of making the hat trick so nearly within his grasp (that of winning distance events in three consecutive Olympics) and condemned him to give up his aspirations while still at his finest. Under international rulings an athlete is forbidden to change countries once having competed in an Olympic event, so that the Australian authorities immobilized Murray completely. In doing so, they also violated the rulings of the International Olympic Committee, which requires that no competitor may neglect his usual employment in order to qualify.

Only those intimately associated with championship sport are able to sincerely comprehend, and so interpret to others, the way in which an athlete must accept the responsibilities entrusted to him. Even his career is frequently hampered by the severe restrictions ruling his amateur status. Surely it is *his* dedication, long-suffering, and his constant, grueling striving which not only create a privileged position for officials but which also bring them honor and esteem. In the same spirit, a dedicated official will do no less than accept his stewardship in its highest sense. He is equally beholden to put the Olympic code before his own self-interest and aggrandizement.

Sooner or later we all meet some impenetrable barrier which seemingly has been formed out of human error of thought or judgment. To us, this was such a barrier—one we strove vainly to remove with words of truth and heartfelt feelings. For a time one is engulfed by hurt and disbelief. In the end such barriers can only be bypassed, or jumped over, then left behind for good.

Perhaps it was Gensei, our little Japanese gardener, who first brought the whole painful incident into clearer focus. "We in Japan," he said gently, "revere the cherry blossom as a symbol of true greatness. These flowers never slowly fade but drop from the tree in the fullness of beauty; that way they are always seen and remembered at the height of their splendor. The sudden change in the affairs of this famed champion puts me very much in mind of our cherry blossom. Is it not good to be remembered splendidly?"

As I look down from my window the afterglow of sunset warmly tinges our everyday scene, and I think of the great wisdom of our little gardener's words.

It is time, I know, when we must break through the limitations of yet another confining shell. One star appears bright and is promisingly reassuring that there is no end—only new beginnings.